Gooseberry Patch co.
Everyday
Cakes, Pies & Cookies

Caramel Cake,
page 13

Gooseberry Patch *Everyday* Cakes, Pies & Cookies

260 recipes for baking sweet memories

OXMOOR HOUSE

Dear Friend,

At the end of a delicious meal, nothing tastes better than the sweet finish of a yummy homemade dessert. But who has the time to make dessert from scratch? With *Gooseberry Patch Everyday Cakes, Pies & Cookies*, you do! We've created 260 simple, soul-satisfying recipes for you and your family to enjoy. From easy-to-bake cookies, decadent layer cakes and homemade pies and tarts to toasty bread puddings and even frozen delights for those warm summer months, these recipes will keep your sweet tooth happy.

For that special occasion, try our Strawberry Layer Cake (page 8)...relish the fresh chopped strawberries in the frosting! For a treat after school, bake up a batch of Chocolate Thumbprint Cookies (page 71) or Peanut Butter Jumbos (page 74) to wow the kiddos. And finally, showcase your baking skills during the holidays with our Maple-Pecan Pie (page 107) or Caramel-Nut Tart (page 138), drizzled in rich melted chocolate.

Indulge yourself with this collection of our tried & true favorite dessert recipes of all time. Passed down from generation to generation, shared with friends, family or neighbors, these recipes will give you something special to bake for every occasion. With *Gooseberry Patch Everyday Cakes, Pies & Cookies,* we guarantee you'll always save room for dessert.

Happy Baking!

Jo Ann & Vickie
co-founders of Gooseberry Patch

contents

Luscious Layer + Other Cakes 6

Crunchy Cookies + Chewy Bars 58

Old-Fashioned Pies, Cobblers + Tarts 102

Homemade Breads + Coffee Cakes 146

Bread Puddings + Custards 184

Frozen Treats 214

Metric Equivalents 250

Index 251

Our Story 256

Italian Cream
Cake, page 27

luscious layer + other cakes

Impress family and friends with this collection of our best cakes. From Blue-Ribbon Chocolate Cake and Praline-Cream Cheese Pound Cake to Raspberry Crunch Cheesecake, there's a recipe for every occasion.

"Spring was always a wonderful time of the year when I was growing up in North Carolina. I remember going with Grandma to the strawberry farm to pick those huge, luscious red berries, often eating as many as we put in the basket!"

—Steven

Strawberry Layer Cake

6-oz. pkg. strawberry gelatin mix
½ c. hot water
18¼-oz. pkg. white cake mix
2 T. all-purpose flour
1 c. strawberries, hulled and chopped
4 eggs

Dissolve dry gelatin mix in hot water in a large bowl; cool. Add dry cake mix, flour and strawberries; mix well. Add eggs, one at a time, beating slightly after each addition. Pour batter into 3 greased and floured 8" round cake pans. Bake at 350 degrees for 20 minutes, or until a toothpick inserted in the center comes out clean. Let cool one hour. Spread Strawberry Frosting between layers and on top and sides of cake. Serves 12.

Strawberry Frosting

¼ c. butter, softened
3¾ to 5 c. powdered sugar
⅓ c. strawberries, hulled and finely chopped

Blend together butter and powdered sugar in a large bowl, adding sugar to desired consistency. Add strawberries; blend thoroughly.

Steven Wilson
Chesterfield, VA

Boston Cream Cake

Drizzled with rich hot fudge…perfect for chocolate lovers!

6 egg whites
½ c. applesauce
18¼-oz. pkg. yellow cake mix
1-oz. pkg. instant sugar-free
  vanilla pudding mix

1½ c. milk
⅔ c. hot fudge topping, divided

Beat egg whites in a large bowl with an electric mixer at high speed 30 seconds. Add applesauce and beat 10 more seconds. Gradually add cake mix. Beat at high speed 2 minutes. Divide and spread batter equally among 4 greased and floured 8" round cake pans. Bake at 350 degrees for 15 minutes, or until a toothpick inserted in the center comes out clean. Cool in pans on wire racks 10 minutes. Remove from pans; cool completely on wire racks.

Beat pudding mix and milk in a medium bowl with an electric mixer at low speed 2 minutes; refrigerate until cakes are completely cooled. To assemble cakes, place one cake layer on a cake plate. Spread half of pudding mixture on cake. Place second cake layer on top of pudding mixture. Spread ⅓ cup hot fudge topping on top of cake. Repeat for third and fourth cake layers. Keep refrigerated until ready to serve. Serves 16.

Sheri Vanderzee
Midland Park, NJ

Red Velvet Cake

This recipe can be used throughout the year for several holidays. For Valentine's Day, bake it in heart-shaped pans, and it's a beautiful Fourth of July cake, too. Of course it's a must at Christmastime.

2½ c. all-purpose flour
1½ c. sugar
1 t. salt
1 t. baking cocoa
1 c. buttermilk
1½ c. oil

2 eggs, beaten
1 t. vanilla extract
1-oz. bottle red food coloring
1 t. white vinegar
1 t. baking soda

Sift together flour, sugar, salt and cocoa in a large bowl. Add buttermilk, oil, eggs and vanilla; mix well. Stir in food coloring. Mix vinegar and baking soda together in a cup. Add to batter; mix only until well blended. Pour into 3 greased and floured 9" round cake pans. Bake at 325 degrees for 30 to 35 minutes, until a toothpick inserted in the center comes out clean. Cool slightly; remove from pans and cool completely on wire racks. Assemble and frost cake with Cream Cheese Frosting. Serves 10 to 12.

Cream Cheese Frosting

8-oz. pkg. cream cheese,
  softened
½ c. margarine

1 t. vanilla extract
6 c. powdered sugar
Optional: ⅓ c. chopped pecans

Blend cream cheese, margarine and vanilla in a large bowl. Stir in powdered sugar until well mixed. Add nuts, if desired.

Peggy Frazier
Indianapolis, IN

Caramel Cake

8-oz. container sour cream
¼ c. milk
1 c. butter, softened
2 c. sugar
4 eggs

2¾ c. all-purpose flour
2 t. baking powder
½ t. salt
1 t. vanilla extract

make-ahead magic

Make the cake layers the day before. Once cool, wrap each layer tightly in plastic wrap.

Combine sour cream and milk in a small bowl; set aside. Beat butter with an electric mixer at medium speed in a large bowl until creamy. Gradually add sugar, beating well. Add eggs, one at a time, beating until blended after each addition. Combine flour, baking powder and salt in a separate bowl; add to butter mixture alternately with sour cream mixture, beginning and ending with flour mixture. Beat at medium-low speed until blended after each addition. Stir in vanilla. Pour batter into 2 greased and floured 9" round cake pans. Bake at 350 degrees for 30 to 35 minutes, until a toothpick inserted in the center comes out clean. Cool in pans on wire racks 10 minutes. Remove from pans to wire racks and let cool one hour, or until completely cool. Spread Whipped Cream Caramel Frosting between layers and on top and sides of cake. Serves 8.

Whipped Cream Caramel Frosting

1 c. butter
2 c. dark brown sugar, packed
¼ c. plus 2 T. whipping cream

2 t. vanilla extract
3¾ c. powdered sugar

Melt butter in a 3-quart saucepan over medium heat. Add brown sugar; bring to a boil, stirring constantly. Stir in whipping cream and vanilla; bring to a boil. Remove from heat; let cool one hour. Transfer to a mixing bowl. Sift powdered sugar into sugar mixture. Beat with an electric mixer at high speed until creamy and spreading consistency. Makes 3¾ cups.

Blue-Ribbon Chocolate Cake

¼ c. butter, softened
¼ c. shortening
2 c. sugar
1 t. vanilla extract
2 eggs

1¾ c. all-purpose flour
¾ c. baking cocoa
¾ t. salt
¼ t. baking powder
1¾ c. milk

Beat butter, shortening, sugar and vanilla in a large bowl until fluffy; blend in eggs and set aside. Combine flour, cocoa, salt and baking powder in a separate bowl; add alternately with milk to sugar mixture. Blend well; pour into 2 greased and floured 9" round cake pans. Bake at 350 degrees for 30 to 35 minutes. Cool in pans on wire racks 10 minutes. Remove from pans to wire racks and let cool one hour, or until completely cool. Spread Frosting between layers and on top and sides of cake. Serves 10 to 12.

Frosting

6 T. butter, softened
½ c. baking cocoa
2⅔ c. powdered sugar

⅓ c. milk
1 t. vanilla extract

Beat butter in a large bowl until fluffy; add cocoa and powdered sugar alternately with milk. Mix in vanilla; blend until smooth and creamy.

Chris Leasure
Radnor, OH

flavor boost

Coffee adds a rich flavor to chocolate recipes…just substitute an equal amount for water or milk in cake, cookie and brownie recipes.

Éclair Cake

Luscious cream filling and chocolatey topping…best with a tall, cold glass of milk.

1 c. water
½ c. butter
1 c. all-purpose flour
4 eggs, beaten
8-oz. pkg. cream cheese, softened

3 c. milk
2 3-oz. pkgs. instant vanilla pudding mix
Garnish: whipped topping, chocolate syrup

Combine water and butter in a saucepan; heat until boiling. Whisk in flour until smooth; remove from heat. Pour mixture into a mixing bowl; gradually blend in eggs. Spread in a greased 13"x9" baking pan; bake at 350 degrees for 30 minutes. Remove from oven; press crust down lightly and set aside. Beat cream cheese, milk and pudding mix in a large bowl 2 minutes; spread over crust. Refrigerate until firm. Top with a layer of whipped topping and drizzle with chocolate syrup before serving. Serves 12 to 15.

Cheryl Frost
Woodstock, OH

Nana's Famous Coconut-Pineapple Cake

The "secret" ingredient in this fabulous family favorite: lemon-lime soda.

15¼-oz. can crushed
   pineapple in juice,
   undrained and divided
1½ c. butter, softened
3 c. sugar
5 eggs

½ c. lemon-lime soda
3 c. cake flour, sifted
1 t. lemon extract
1 t. vanilla extract
6-oz. pkg. frozen sweetened
   flaked coconut, thawed

Drain pineapple, reserving ¾ cup juice. Remove ¼ cup reserved juice for Cream Cheese Frosting, and reserve crushed pineapple for Pineapple Filling.

Beat butter in a large bowl with an electric mixer at medium speed until creamy; gradually add sugar, beating well. Add eggs, one at a time, beating until blended after each addition. Combine ½ cup reserved pineapple juice and lemon-lime soda. Add flour to butter mixture alternately with juice mixture, beginning and ending with flour. Beat at low speed until blended after each addition. Stir in extracts. Pour batter into 3 greased and floured 9" round cake pans lined with wax paper. Bake at 350 degrees for 25 to 30 minutes, until a toothpick inserted near the center comes out clean. Remove from pans immediately; cool on wire racks one hour.

Spread ¾ cup Pineapple Filling between cake layers; spread remaining filling on top of cake. Spread Cream Cheese Frosting on sides of cake. Sprinkle top and sides of cake with coconut. Serves 10 to 12.

Pineapple Filling

2 c. sugar
¼ c. cornstarch
1 c. water

1 c. reserved crushed
   pineapple, drained

Stir together sugar and cornstarch in a medium saucepan. Stir in water and pineapple. Cook over low heat, stirring occasionally, 15 minutes, or until mixture is thickened. Let cool completely.

Cream Cheese Frosting

½ c. butter, softened
3-oz. pkg. cream cheese, softened
16-oz. pkg. powdered sugar, sifted
¼ c. reserved pineapple juice
1 t. vanilla extract

Beat butter and cream cheese with an electric mixer at medium speed until creamy. Gradually add powdered sugar, juice and vanilla; mix well.

Double-Chocolate Mousse Cake

Don't believe in a flourless cake? Try this!

16-oz. pkg. semi-sweet chocolate chips
2 c. butter
1 c. sugar
1 c. half-and-half
½ t. salt
1 T. vanilla extract
8 eggs, lightly beaten
Garnish: whipped topping

Place chocolate chips, butter, sugar, half-and-half, salt and vanilla in a heavy saucepan; heat over low heat, stirring frequently, until chocolate chips melt. Cool to room temperature; fold in eggs. Pour into a greased 9" springform pan; bake at 350 degrees for 45 minutes. Cool to room temperature; spread with Topping. Refrigerate until firm; carefully remove sides of pan. Garnish with whipped topping before serving. Serves 10 to 12.

Topping

1 c. chocolate chips
2 T. butter
3 T. half-and-half
2 T. corn syrup

Melt chocolate chips with butter in a double boiler; remove from heat. Stir in half-and-half and corn syrup; mix until smooth.

Jessica Jones
York, PA

Old-Fashioned Jam Cake

For neat slices, cut with an electric knife.

1 c. plus 6 T. shortening, divided	1 t. baking soda
5¾ c. sugar, divided	½ t. salt
½ c. water	1 t. each cinnamon, allspice and nutmeg
½ c. applesauce	1 c. buttermilk
1 c. seedless blackberry jam	1 c. raisins
2 eggs	1 c. chopped pecans
3 c. all-purpose flour	6 T. butter
½ c. baking cocoa	1½ c. milk
1 t. baking powder	1½ t. vanilla extract

Beat one cup shortening in a large bowl until creamy; gradually beat in 2 cups sugar. Add water; beat until fluffy. Beat in applesauce and jam; add eggs, one at a time, beating until blended after each addition. Combine flour, cocoa, baking powder, baking soda, salt and spices in a separate bowl; add to shortening mixture alternately with buttermilk. Stir in raisins and pecans. Pour into 3 lightly greased 9" round cake pans. Bake at 350 degrees for 24 minutes, or until a toothpick inserted in the center comes out clean. Cool in pans 10 minutes; remove from pans and cool completely on wire racks.

Combine 3 cups sugar, remaining shortening, butter and milk in a heavy saucepan. Bring to a boil; remove from heat. Heat remaining sugar in a separate saucepan over medium heat until sugar melts and is golden. Stirring rapidly, pour into shortening mixture in saucepan; bring to a boil over medium heat. Cook, stirring constantly, about 15 minutes, until icing reaches soft-ball stage, or 234 to 243 degrees on a candy thermometer. Remove from heat; stir in vanilla. Let stand 10 minutes, then beat icing with a wooden spoon until thick and creamy but still hot. Spread frosting between layers and on sides and top of cake; smooth with a spatula dipped in hot water, if necessary. Serves 12.

Mandarin Orange Cake

My daughter's favorite cake…the one she always requests for her birthday!

18½-oz. pkg. white cake mix
11-oz. can mandarin oranges,
   drained and juice reserved
3 egg whites
½ c. oil
2 8-oz. cans crushed pineapple

3½-oz. pkg. instant vanilla
   pudding mix
8-oz. container frozen whipped
   topping, thawed
1 c. sweetened flaked
   coconut, divided

Combine cake mix, reserved juice, egg whites and oil in a large bowl.
Beat with an electric mixer at medium speed 2 minutes, or until creamy.
Fold in oranges; pour into a greased and floured 13"x9" baking pan. Bake
at 350 degrees for 25 to 35 minutes, until a toothpick inserted in the
center comes out clean. Place pan on a wire rack to cool completely. Pour
pineapple and its juice into a medium bowl; stir in pudding mix. Fold in
whipped topping and ½ cup coconut. Mix well; chill while cake is cooling.
Spread frosting over top of cake; sprinkle with remaining coconut. Serve
immediately or keep refrigerated. Serves 12.

Nancy Likens
Wooster, OH

Oatmeal Cake

> "I remember this recipe as a dessert that my mother prepared on many occasions. Everyone would always compliment her. Now that I've continued the tradition, I'm the one getting the compliments…but I owe it all to her."
>
> —Teresa

1 c. oats
1½ c. boiling water
½ c. butter, softened
1 c. sugar
1 c. brown sugar, packed

2 eggs
⅛ t. salt
1½ c. all-purpose flour
1 t. baking soda
1 t. cinnamon

Mix oats and boiling water in a bowl. Let stand 20 minutes. Beat butter and sugars in a large bowl. Add eggs and salt; stir in oatmeal. Stir in flour, baking soda and cinnamon. Pour into a greased and floured 13"x9" baking pan. Bake at 325 degrees for 35 minutes. Spoon Icing over warm cake. Place cake under broiler until bubbly. Serves 10 to 12.

Icing

¾ c. butter, softened
1 c. brown sugar, packed
½ c. half-and-half

1 c. chopped pecans
1 c. flaked coconut

Mix together all ingredients in a bowl until smooth.

Teresa Cates
Odessa, TX

Honey Bun Cake

18¼-oz. pkg. yellow cake mix
4 eggs, beaten
¾ c. oil
1 c. buttermilk

1 c. brown sugar, packed
2 t. cinnamon
½ c. chopped pecans

"Our family loves this cake!"

—Carol

Combine cake mix, eggs, oil and buttermilk in a large bowl; mix well. Pour into a greased 13"x9" baking pan. Combine brown sugar, cinnamon and pecans in a small bowl. Swirl into batter. Bake at 300 degrees for 40 to 60 minutes, until a toothpick inserted in the center comes out clean. Pour Glaze over warm cake. Serves 10 to 12.

Glaze

1 c. powdered sugar
2 T. milk

1 t. vanilla extract

Mix all ingredients in a bowl until smooth.

Carol Lankford
Danville, LA

Strawberry Shortcake

Very, very simple and looks so pretty!

2 c. all-purpose flour
3 t. baking powder
½ t. salt
½ c. sugar
⅓ c. butter, melted
1 c. milk
Garnish: sliced and whole
    strawberries, half-and-half

Combine dry ingredients in a large bowl; stir in butter and milk. Spread in a greased 13"x9" baking pan. Bake at 450 degrees for 12 to 15 minutes; cool. Cut into squares; slice horizontally. Spoon sliced strawberries onto bottom slice of each cake square; pour one tablespoon half-and-half over the strawberries. Top with remaining slice; garnish with a whole strawberry. Serves 12 to 15.

T.R. Ralston
Gooseberry Patch

Warm Turtle Cake

"This cake reminds me of the boxes of chocolate-covered turtles that my dad used to bring home for us when we were little!"

—Laurie

18¼-oz. pkg. Swiss chocolate
    cake mix
⅓ c. plus ½ c. evaporated
    milk, divided
¾ c. butter, melted
14-oz. pkg. caramels,
    unwrapped
1 c. pecan pieces
¾ c. chocolate chips

Beat cake mix, ⅓ cup evaporated milk and melted butter in a large bowl with an electric mixer at medium speed 2 minutes. Pour half of mixture into a greased 11"x7" baking pan. Bake at 350 degrees for 6 minutes. Melt ½ cup evaporated milk and caramels in a double boiler over medium heat. Drizzle over cake. Sprinkle pecan pieces and chocolate chips over caramel. Use a wet knife to spread the remaining cake mixture over the pecan pieces and chocolate chips. Bake at 350 degrees for 18 minutes. Serves 12.

Laurie Benham
Playas, NM

Warm Turtle Cake

Texas Sheet Cake

Round up your family and friends for this wonderful Texas-size cake.

1 c. margarine	½ t. salt
1 c. water	2 eggs, beaten
6 T. baking cocoa	8-oz. container sour cream
2 c. all-purpose flour	1 t. baking soda
2 c. sugar	Garnish: chopped walnuts
½ t. cinnamon	

Combine margarine, water and cocoa in a saucepan over medium heat. Bring to a boil; remove from heat. Mix flour, sugar, cinnamon and salt in a large bowl; stir in hot mixture. Mix remaining ingredients except nuts in a separate bowl; add to batter and mix well. Pour into a greased 15"x10" jelly-roll pan. Bake at 350 degrees for 22 minutes. Pour Icing over hot cake; sprinkle with nuts. Serves 20.

Icing

½ c. margarine	16-oz. pkg. powdered sugar
¼ c. baking cocoa	1 t. vanilla extract
6 T. milk	

Bring margarine, cocoa and milk to a boil in a saucepan over medium-high heat; remove from heat. Stir in powdered sugar and vanilla.

Doris Stegner
Gooseberry Patch

tasty twist

Top with any chopped nuts! Try pecans, almonds or even hazelnuts.

Three-Layer Chocolate Cake

A chocolate lover's dream dessert.

1 c. butter, softened	1 c. baking cocoa
1¾ c. sugar	1½ t. baking powder
1 T. vanilla extract	1 t. baking soda
3 eggs	¼ t. salt
2¼ c. all-purpose flour	1¾ c. milk

Beat butter, sugar and vanilla in a large mixing bowl until light and fluffy. Add eggs; beat well and set aside. Sift together all dry ingredients in a separate bowl and alternately add with milk to sugar mixture. Divide evenly into 3 greased 9" round cake pans; bake at 350 degrees for 25 to 30 minutes. Cool 10 minutes in pans. Remove from pans to wire racks to cool completely. Spread Fudge Frosting between layers and on top and sides of cake. Serves 12.

Fudge Frosting

1 c. butter, softened	2 t. vanilla extract
4 c. powdered sugar	4 to 5 T. milk
½ c. baking cocoa	

Combine all ingredients in a large mixing bowl; beat with an electric mixer until smooth.

Pam Vienneau
Derby, CT

Italian Cream Cake

2 c. sugar
½ c. butter, softened
½ c. shortening
½ c. buttermilk
2 c. all-purpose flour
1 t. baking soda
½ t. salt
5 eggs, separated
1 c. chopped pecans
2 c. flaked coconut
Garnish: flaked coconut
   and chopped pecans

Combine sugar, butter, shortening and buttermilk in a large mixing bowl; set aside. Mix flour, baking soda and salt in a separate mixing bowl; set aside. Alternately, add the flour mixture and the egg yolks to the sugar mixture, blending well. Stir in pecans and coconut; set aside. Beat egg whites in a small bowl until stiff. Fold into batter and pour into 2 greased and floured 8" round cake pans. Bake at 350 degrees for 20 to 30 minutes. Remove from pans to wire racks to cool completely. Spread Frosting between layers and on top and sides of cake. Sprinkle with coconut and pecans. Serves 8.

Frosting

8-oz. pkg. cream cheese,
   softened
½ c. butter, softened
1 t. vanilla extract
¾ t. butter flavoring
16-oz. pkg. powdered sugar

Beat all ingredients in a large bowl until smooth.

Kim Schooler
Norman, OK

"A tried & true recipe handed down from Grandma."

—Kim

Praline Pound Cake

Unbelievably good served with a side of vanilla ice cream.

1 lb. **butter**, softened	4 c. **all-purpose flour**
2 c. **sugar**	¾ c. **pecans**, finely chopped
1 c. **brown sugar**, packed	¾ c. **milk**
6 **eggs**	1 T. **vanilla extract**

Beat butter and sugars in a large bowl; add eggs, one at a time, beating well after each addition. Toss flour with pecans in a separate bowl. Alternate adding flour mixture and milk to butter mixture, beginning and ending with flour. Stir in vanilla; beat batter 5 minutes. Pour into a greased and floured 10" tube pan; bake at 325 degrees for 1½ hours. Cool in pan 15 minutes; remove from pan to a wire rack. Poke holes in top of cake with a fork. Drizzle Glaze over cake. Serves 12.

Glaze

1 c. **brown sugar**, packed	½ c. **butter**
1 c. **chopped pecans**	

Combine ingredients in a saucepan; bring to a boil over medium heat. Stir until smooth.

Beth Livengood
Landis, NC

neat trick

If a recipe calls for a tube pan and there's not one handy, make your own. Set a clean empty can in the middle of a deep cake pan. Fill the can with beans to keep it in place, then carefully pour the batter around the can... so simple!

Brown Sugar Pound Cake

1 c. butter, softened
1 c. brown sugar, packed
1 t. vanilla extract
4 eggs, beaten
1½ c. plus 2 T. all-purpose flour
1½ t. baking powder
½ t. salt

Beat butter and brown sugar in a bowl until light and fluffy; mix in vanilla. Blend in eggs. Combine flour, baking powder and salt in a large bowl; blend in egg mixture. Spread batter in a greased and floured 9"x5" glass loaf pan; bake at 350 degrees for one hour and 10 minutes, or until a toothpick inserted in the center comes out clean. Cool in pan on a wire rack one hour; remove from pan to wire rack to cool completely. Serves 8.

Kathy Grashoff
Fort Wayne, IN

Cherry-Chocolate Marble Cake

1 c. margarine, softened
2 c. sugar
3 eggs
6 T. maraschino cherry juice
6 T. water
2 t. almond extract
3¾ c. all-purpose flour
2¼ t. baking soda
¾ t. salt
1½ c. sour cream
¾ c. maraschino cherries, drained and chopped
¾ c. chopped walnuts
3 1-oz. sqs. unsweetened baking chocolate, melted
Garnish: powdered sugar

Blend margarine and sugar in a large bowl; add eggs, blending after each addition. Mix in juice, water and almond extract. Combine flour, baking soda and salt in a separate bowl; blend into sugar mixture alternately with sour cream. Place half the batter in another mixing bowl; stir in cherries and walnuts. Blend chocolate into remaining batter. Spoon half the cherry batter into a greased 10" tube pan; spoon half the chocolate batter on top. Repeat layers. Bake at 350 degrees for one hour and 15 minutes, or until a toothpick inserted in the center comes out clean. Cool in pan 30 minutes; remove and cool completely. Sprinkle with powdered sugar. Serves 15 to 18.

Sharon Webb
Clinton, IL

Angel Food Cake
Lori Burris (Gooseberry Patch)

When time allows, make this heavenly cake from scratch…it's so much simpler than you think.

10 egg whites
½ t. salt
1½ t. cream of tartar

1½ t. vanilla extract
1¼ c. cake flour
1¾ c. sugar

Beat egg whites and salt in a large bowl with an electric mixer at high speed until foamy; add cream of tartar and vanilla, beating until soft peaks form. Combine flour and sugar in a separate bowl; add to egg white mixture, beating well. Fold into an ungreased 10" tube pan; draw knife through batter to remove air bubbles. Bake at 375 degrees for 30 to 40 minutes, until top springs back when pressed. Invert pan, placing center over top of a bottle; cool one hour, then remove cake from pan. Serves 12 to 16.

Rich Spice Cake

"A family favorite from one of my grandmother's oldest cookbooks, dated 1928."

—Naomi

2 c. plus 1 T. all-purpose flour, divided
2 t. cinnamon
1 t. ground cloves
1 t. allspice
½ t. nutmeg
1 t. baking soda
1 c. less 2 T. milk
2 T. vinegar
½ c. shortening
2 c. brown sugar, packed
3 egg yolks, beaten
2 egg whites, stiffly beaten
1 c. raisins

Sift together 2 cups flour, cinnamon, cloves, allspice, nutmeg and baking soda in a bowl; set aside. Stir together milk and vinegar in a small bowl; set aside. Beat shortening and sugar in a large mixing bowl; add egg yolks. Gradually stir in flour mixture alternately with milk mixture; fold in egg whites. Toss raisins with remaining flour in a small bowl; fold into batter. Pour into 2 greased 8" round cake pans; bake at 350 degrees for 30 minutes, or until a toothpick inserted into the center comes out clean. Remove from pans to wire racks to cool completely. Frost with Caramel Icing. Serves 8 to 12.

Caramel Icing

2 c. brown sugar, packed
1 c. whipping cream
1 T. butter
1 t. vanilla extract

Cook brown sugar and cream in a heavy saucepan over medium-high heat until soft-ball stage, or 234 to 240 degrees on a candy thermometer. Stir in butter and vanilla; remove from heat. Beat until desired spreading consistency is reached.

Naomi Cycak
Ligonier, PA

Summertime Strawberry Shortcake

3 to 4 c. strawberries, hulled
and sliced
½ c. plus 2 T. sugar, divided
2 c. all-purpose flour
1 T. baking powder
½ t. salt
¾ c. butter, divided
1 egg, beaten
⅔ c. light cream
1 c. whipping cream, whipped

Toss strawberries with ½ cup sugar in a bowl and set aside. Combine flour, remaining sugar, baking powder and salt in a separate bowl. Cut in ½ cup butter until mixture forms coarse crumbs; set aside. Whisk together egg and light cream in a small bowl; add to flour mixture, stirring just until moistened. Divide dough into 6 parts; pat into biscuits and place on a greased baking sheet. Bake at 450 degrees for 8 to 10 minutes, until golden. Cool biscuits briefly on a wire rack. Split in half with a serrated knife; spread bottoms with remaining butter. Top with berries and whipped cream; add tops. Garnish with remaining berries and cream. Serves 6.

Martha Doyle
Rome, NY

tasty twist

Try your favorite berry instead of the strawberries.

quick & easy

Make one big shortcake! Pat dough into a greased 8" round cake pan and bake at 450 degrees for 15 to 18 minutes.

Raspberry Upside-Down
Cake

Raspberry Upside-Down Cake

Great served warm or cold, and it couldn't be easier to prepare!

18¼-oz. pkg. yellow cake mix
1 c. raspberries
¾ c. sugar
½ c. whipping cream
Garnish: powdered sugar

Prepare cake mix according to package directions. Pour into 2 greased and floured 9" round cake pans. Place raspberries over top of cake batter. Sprinkle sugar over raspberries. Gently pour whipping cream over top. Bake at 350 degrees for 25 to 35 minutes. Let stand 10 minutes. Turn upside down on a plate to serve. Sprinkle with powdered sugar. Serves 16.

Becky Rogers
Saline, MI

kitchen tip

To avoid overbaking, set your timer for 3 minutes fewer than the allotted time.

Vanilla Wafer Cake

This is best enjoyed with good friends and coffee.

1 c. butter, softened
2 c. sugar
6 eggs
12-oz. pkg. vanilla wafers, crushed
1 c. pecans, chopped
½ c. milk
1 t. vanilla extract

Blend butter and sugar in a large bowl. Add eggs, one at a time, beating after each addition. Add vanilla wafers, pecans, milk and vanilla. Pour into a greased and floured Bundt® pan. Bake at 325 degrees for 1½ hours; let cool before removing from pan. Serves 8.

Margie Scott
Winnsboro, TX

Nobby Apple Cake
Lynn Williams (Muncie, IN)

This tasty recipe was found in a very old farmers' cookbook.

3 T. butter, softened
1 c. sugar
1 egg, beaten
1 c. all-purpose flour
1 t. baking soda
½ t. salt

½ t. cinnamon
½ t. nutmeg
3 c. apples, peeled, cored and diced
¼ c. nuts, chopped
1 t. vanilla extract

Blend butter and sugar in a large bowl. Stir in egg until well blended. Sift together dry ingredients in a separate bowl; add to butter mixture. Fold in apples and nuts; stir in vanilla. Pour into an oiled 8"x8" baking pan; bake at 350 degrees for 40 to 45 minutes. Serves 6.

Root Beer Cake

Yes, it sounds unusual, but it's wonderful!

1 c. sugar
½ c. butter, softened
½ t. vanilla extract
2 eggs

2 c. all-purpose flour
1 T. baking powder
1 t. salt
⅔ c. root beer

Combine all ingredients in a large mixing bowl. Beat with an electric mixer at low speed; beat at medium speed 3 minutes. Pour into a greased and floured 12"x8" baking pan. Bake at 375 degrees for 30 to 35 minutes. Spread Frosting on cooled cake. Serves 8.

Frosting

16-oz. pkg. powdered sugar

1 c. root beer, chilled

Combine ingredients in a mixing bowl and blend well. Beat until thick and fluffy.

Tish DeYoung
Wausau, WI

kitchen tip

Soften your butter quickly by cutting it into very small pieces. It will soften in no time!

Fudge Cake

If you're craving chocolate, try this! The peanut butter gives it a special flavor.

2 c. all-purpose flour
2 c. sugar
1½ c. margarine, divided
½ c. baking cocoa, divided
1 c. water
½ c. buttermilk
2 eggs
1 t. baking soda
½ t. cinnamon
2 t. vanilla extract, divided
1 c. peanut butter
1 t. oil
5 T. milk
16-oz. pkg. powdered sugar
2 4-oz. pkgs. chopped nuts
Garnish: chopped peanuts

Sift together flour and sugar in a large bowl; set aside. Combine one cup margarine, ¼ cup cocoa and water in a saucepan; bring to a rapid boil and let cool. Pour cocoa mixture over flour mixture; beat. Add buttermilk, eggs, baking soda, cinnamon and one teaspoon vanilla, beating after each addition. Pour mixture into a greased and floured 13"x9" glass baking pan. Bake at 350 degrees for 25 to 30 minutes; let cool. Mix peanut butter and oil in a small bowl; spread on cooled cake. Place in refrigerator until peanut butter is chilled. Mix remaining margarine, remaining cocoa and milk in a saucepan; bring to a boil. Boil 2 minutes; remove from heat. Beat in powdered sugar, remaining vanilla and nuts. Spread over cooled cake. Garnish with peanuts. Serves 10 to 12.

Jane Fleming
Elkview, WV

in a pinch

If you don't have time to frost a cake, you can give it an extra-special look in no time! Just lay a cake stencil over the top of a baked cake…they come in all kinds of pretty patterns. Sprinkle with powdered sugar or cocoa, then gently remove the stencil to show your pattern.

Chocolate-Pumpkin Pound Cake

3 c. all-purpose flour
1 T. pumpkin pie spice
2 t. baking powder
1 t. baking soda
½ t. salt
1 c. butter or margarine, softened
1⅓ c. brown sugar, packed

1 c. sugar
4 eggs
15-oz. can pumpkin
2 t. vanilla extract
½ c. milk
1¼ c. semisweet chocolate chips, divided

Combine flour, pumpkin pie spice, baking powder, baking soda and salt in a medium bowl; set aside. Beat butter and sugars in a large bowl with an electric mixer at medium speed until creamy. Add eggs, one at a time, beating at low speed after each addition until blended. Add pumpkin and vanilla; beat at medium speed until blended. Beat in flour mixture alternately with milk at low speed until smooth. Stir in one cup chocolate chips. Spoon batter into a greased and lightly floured 10" tube pan. Bake at 350 degrees for 55 to 60 minutes, until a toothpick inserted in the center comes out clean. Cool in pan 10 minutes; remove from pan to a wire rack and cool completely, about one hour. Drizzle Glaze over cake. Sprinkle with remaining ¼ cup chocolate chips. Serves 16.

Glaze

1½ c. powdered sugar
2 to 3 T. milk

½ t. vanilla extract

Combine all ingredients in a medium bowl until smooth and thick.

Praline-Cream Cheese Pound Cake

"My favorite because it has a rich caramel flavor that satisfies my most urgent sweet tooth!"

—Vicki

1 c. butter, softened
8-oz. pkg. cream cheese, softened
16-oz. pkg. brown sugar
1 c. sugar
5 eggs

3½ c. cake flour
½ t. baking powder
½ c. milk
1½ t. vanilla extract
1 c. pecans, chopped

Blend butter and cream cheese in a large bowl. Add brown sugar and sugar, one cup at a time, beating until light and fluffy. Add eggs, one at a time, beating well after each addition. Sift together flour and baking powder and add to butter mixture alternately with milk, beginning and ending with flour mixture. Add vanilla and nuts; mix well. Pour into a greased and floured 10" tube pan. Bake at 300 degrees for 2 hours, or until a toothpick inserted in the center comes out clean. Cool in pan 10 minutes; remove from pan to a wire rack and cool completely. Spread with Frosting. Serves 10.

Frosting

3 c. sugar, divided
½ c. water
1 egg, beaten
1 c. milk

½ c. butter
1 t. vinegar
⅛ t. salt

Place ½ cup sugar in a heavy skillet. Cook over low heat, stirring constantly, until melted and brown. Add water and stir until dissolved. Add remaining sugar. Mix egg with milk in a small bowl and stir into sugar mixture. Add butter, vinegar and salt. Cook to soft-ball stage, or 234 to 240 degrees on a candy thermometer; cool. Beat until frosting reaches desired spreading consistency.

Vicki Jones
Rutherfordton, NC

Toffee & Black Walnut Cake

Crunchy walnuts and toffee bars are the filling for this sugar-dusted cake. Served warm from the oven, it'll disappear quickly!

2 c. all-purpose flour
1¼ c. sugar, divided
1½ t. baking powder
1 t. baking soda
½ t. salt
1½ t. vanilla extract
1 c. sour cream
½ c. butter, softened

2 eggs
1 c. chopped black walnuts, divided
2 t. cinnamon
3 1.4-oz. chocolate-covered toffee candy bars, chopped
¼ c. butter, melted
Garnish: powdered sugar

Combine flour, one cup sugar, baking powder, baking soda, salt, vanilla, sour cream, softened butter, eggs and ½ cup walnuts in a large bowl; beat with an electric mixer at low speed 3 minutes. Pour half the batter into a greased and floured 10" Bundt® pan; set aside. Combine remaining sugar and cinnamon in a small bowl; sprinkle half over the batter. Repeat layers. Combine remaining walnuts and toffee bars in a bowl; sprinkle over the top. Drizzle with melted butter; bake at 325 degrees for 45 to 50 minutes. Cool upright 15 minutes; invert cake onto a serving plate and remove pan. Dust with powdered sugar before serving. Serves 12 to 16.

Janet Pastrick
Gooseberry Patch

kitchen tip

Use a strainer to dust cakes, pies and other confections with powdered sugar.

wow Mom!

Mom will love a spring bonnet cake! Use a round oven-proof bowl to bake the batter in, then cool and invert cake on a cake stand. Line with sugar cookies around the edge for the brim, and then frost and decorate.

Tutti-Frutti Cake

Just a little taste of chocolate really adds something special to this cake.

1 c. sugar
1½ c. all-purpose flour
1 t. baking soda
¼ t. salt
1 c. less 1 T. milk
2 T. lemon juice
½ c. butter, melted

1-oz. sq. baking chocolate, melted
1 egg, beaten
1½ c. chopped dates
½ c. chopped walnuts
1 t. vanilla extract

Combine sugar, flour, baking soda and salt in a large bowl; set aside. Stir together milk and lemon juice in a small bowl; add to flour mixture. Blend in remaining ingredients in order listed; mix well after each addition. Pour into a greased and floured 13"x9" baking pan. Bake at 350 degrees for 35 to 40 minutes. Serves 12.

Michelle Lamp
Slayton, MN

Nutty Raisin Cake

Spread slices with softened cream cheese…so good.

1 c. less 1 T. milk
2 T. lemon juice
1 c. brown sugar, packed
½ c. oil
1 t. baking soda
1 t. nutmeg

¾ c. raisins
2 c. all-purpose flour
1 t. cinnamon
½ t. ground cloves
½ c. chopped nuts

Stir together milk and lemon juice in a large mixing bowl; blend in remaining ingredients. Pour into a greased 9"x5" loaf pan; bake at 350 degrees for one hour, or until a toothpick inserted into the center comes out clean. Serves 8.

Roxanne Bixby
West Franklin, NH

Peanut Butter Sheet Cake

½ c. creamy peanut butter
½ c. butter
½ c. applesauce
1 c. water
2 c. sugar

2 c. all-purpose flour
2 eggs
½ c. milk
1 t. baking soda
1 t. vanilla extract

Combine peanut butter, butter, applesauce and water in a saucepan; bring to a boil. Remove from heat; mix in remaining ingredients. Pour into a lightly greased 15"x10" jelly-roll pan; bake at 350 degrees for 20 to 25 minutes. Cool; frost with Peanut Butter Icing. Serves 24 to 30.

Peanut Butter Icing

½ c. creamy peanut butter
½ c. butter
⅓ c. milk

16-oz. pkg. powdered sugar
1 t. vanilla extract

Place peanut butter, butter and milk in a saucepan; bring to a boil. Remove from heat; blend in powdered sugar and vanilla until smooth and creamy.

Michelle Beal
Parkersburg, WV

"An easy-to-make recipe of my father's that's so good."

—Michelle

sweet presentation

No time to bake? Slice a store-bought pound cake into four layers, spreading raspberry jam between each layer. A topping of freshly whipped cream, whole berries and chocolate curls makes this oh-so-simple dessert delicious!

Chocolate-Chip Cheesecake

24 chocolate sandwich cookies, crushed
¼ c. butter, melted
3 8-oz. pkgs. cream cheese, softened
14-oz. can sweetened condensed milk
3 eggs
1 c. mini chocolate chips
1 T. all-purpose flour
1 t. vanilla extract

Mix together cookies and butter in a bowl and pat into a greased 9" springform pan. Beat remaining ingredients in a bowl and pour on top of crust. Bake at 300 degrees about one hour, or until firm. Cool, then refrigerate. Serves 12.

Jackie Hoover
Newark, OH

Creamy Amaretto Cheesecake

1¼ c. coconut or vanilla wafer cookies, finely crushed
½ c. almonds, ground
6 T. butter, melted
3 8-oz. pkgs. cream cheese, softened
1 c. sugar
¼ t. salt
½ t. almond extract
1 c. sour cream
3 eggs
¼ c. amaretto liqueur

Combine cookies, almonds and butter in a bowl; mix well. Press into the bottom and sides of a lightly buttered 8" springform pan. Bake at 350 degrees for 10 minutes. Beat cream cheese with an electric mixer at medium speed until smooth. Add sugar, salt and almond extract. Beat 3 more minutes. Beat in sour cream. Add eggs, one at a time, beating after each addition. Slowly beat in the amaretto. Beat until well blended. Pour on top of crust and bake at 350 degrees for one hour and 10 minutes, or until golden and set. Turn off oven, leaving oven door slightly open. Let stand in oven for one to 2 hours. Remove from oven, cover with aluminum foil and refrigerate overnight. Serves 12.

Judy Borecky
Escondido, CA

Chocolate Chip
Cheesecake

Cookie Dough Cheesecake

Who can resist cookie dough? Indulge in this!

1¾ c. chocolate chip cookie crumbs
1½ c. sugar, divided
⅓ c. plus ¼ c. butter, melted and divided
3 8-oz. pkgs. cream cheese, softened
3 eggs
8 oz. sour cream
1½ t. vanilla extract, divided
¼ c. brown sugar, packed
1 T. water
½ c. all-purpose flour
1½ c. mini semi-sweet chocolate chips, divided

Combine cookie crumbs and ¼ cup sugar in a small bowl; stir in ⅓ cup butter. Press into bottom and slightly up sides of an ungreased 9" spring-form pan; set aside. Beat cream cheese and one cup sugar in a mixing bowl with an electric mixer until smooth. Add eggs; beat at low speed just until combined. Add sour cream and ½ teaspoon vanilla; beat just until blended. Pour over crust; set aside. Beat remaining butter, remaining ¼ cup sugar and brown sugar in a separate bowl at medium speed 3 minutes. Add water and remaining vanilla; gradually add flour and stir in one cup chocolate chips. Drop by teaspoonfuls over filling, gently pushing dough below surface. Bake at 350 degrees for 45 to 55 minutes, until center is almost set. Cool in pan on a wire rack 10 minutes. Carefully run a knife around edge of pan to loosen; cool one hour longer. Refrigerate overnight. Remove sides of pan and sprinkle cheesecake with remaining chips. Serves 12.

Valarie Dobbins
Edmond, OK

Harvest Apple Cheesecake

2 c. graham cracker crumbs
⅓ c. brown sugar, packed
½ c. butter, melted and divided
1 T. cinnamon
3 apples, peeled, cored and
  sliced into 12 rings
4 eggs
¾ c. sugar
8 oz. ricotta cheese
8-oz. pkg. cream cheese,
  softened
2 t. vanilla extract
8 oz. whipping cream
Garnish: cinnamon

Combine cracker crumbs, brown sugar, ¼ cup butter and cinnamon in a bowl. Press on bottom and part of the way up the sides of an ungreased 9" springform pan. Sauté apple slices on both sides in remaining ¼ cup butter in a skillet over medium heat until caramelized. Arrange 6 apple slices on prepared crust. Beat eggs, sugar, ricotta, cream cheese and vanilla in a bowl until smooth. Add whipping cream and blend. Pour cheese mixture into pan over apple slices. Arrange remaining 6 apple slices on top and press apples slightly under the mixture. Sprinkle top generously with cinnamon. Bake at 450 degrees for 10 minutes; reduce heat to 300 degrees and bake for 50 to 55 minutes. Cool and refrigerate overnight. Serves 12.

Richard Welsch
Delaware, OH

"It's just not autumn until our family takes a trip to the local apple orchard. This cake is the first thing we bake with the fresh apples!"

—Richard

pint-size fun

Serving milk in vintage pint-size milk bottles adds fun to family dessert time!

Raspberry Crunch Cheesecake

Make this the night before...a great time-saver!

2 c. quick-cooking oats, uncooked
2 c. brown sugar, packed
2 c. all-purpose flour
1 c. butter
1 c. nuts, chopped
5 8-oz. pkgs. cream cheese, softened
1 c. sugar
¼ c. cornstarch
½ c. whipping cream
4 eggs
10-oz. jar seedless raspberry jam

Mix together oats, brown sugar and flour in a large bowl. Cut in butter to make crumbs; stir in nuts. Press three-fourths of mixture into the bottom and halfway up the sides of an ungreased 10" springform pan. Bake at 350 degrees for 12 to 15 minutes, until crust is set. Save remaining crumbs for top of cake. Beat cream cheese, sugar, cornstarch and whipping cream in a large bowl with an electric mixer. Add eggs, one at a time, beating well after each addition. Pour into prepared crust. Bake at 350 degrees for 45 minutes. Heat jam in microwave; pour over hot cake and top with reserved crumbs. Return to oven and bake 15 to 20 minutes, until crust is golden brown. Turn off oven and let cake stand in oven one hour. Chill overnight. Serves 12.

Debi Timperley
Stanton, NE

Classic Cheesecake

So versatile…top with blackberries, cherries or kiwi slices.

1¼ c. graham cracker crumbs
¼ c. sugar
1 t. cinnamon

¼ c. butter, melted
1 pt. strawberries, hulled and sliced

Mix all ingredients except strawberries in a small mixing bowl; press firmly into the bottom of a lightly greased 9" springform pan. Pour Filling onto crust; bake at 300 degrees for one hour and 15 minutes. Cover and refrigerate 4 hours before serving. Top with strawberries. Serves 12.

Filling

4 8-oz. pkgs. cream cheese, softened
1 c. sugar

4 eggs
2 t. lemon juice
1 t. vanilla extract

Beat cream cheese in a bowl until creamy; gradually add sugar, blending well. Add eggs, one at a time, mixing well after each addition; stir in lemon juice and vanilla.

Liz Moore
Plano, TX

kitchen tip

Bite-size cheesecakes always disappear fast at potlucks. Any favorite recipe can be used…just bake in mini muffin pans!

No-Bake Cheesecake

What could be easier?

2½ c. graham cracker crumbs
1 c. butter, melted
2 8-oz. pkgs. cream cheese, softened
2 c. sour cream
4 t. vanilla extract
⅔ c. sugar
16-oz. container frozen whipped topping, thawed
Garnish: 21-oz. can cherry pie filling

Toss together graham cracker crumbs and butter in a bowl; press evenly into an ungreased 13"x9" baking pan. Blend cream cheese in a bowl until smooth; stir in sour cream, vanilla and sugar. Fold in whipped topping; spread evenly into crust. Refrigerate overnight. Garnish with pie filling before serving. Serves 12.

Gail Bellman
Pewaukee, WI

No-Bake Strawberry Cheesecake

This easy version is ready to enjoy in no time at all!

kitchen tip

Dress up plain cheesecake in a jiffy! Drizzle slices with warm raspberry preserves.

4 oz. cream cheese, softened
¼ c. sugar
½ c. sour cream
1 t. vanilla extract
4 oz. frozen whipped topping, thawed
1 c. strawberry glaze
9-inch graham cracker crust
1 pt. strawberries, thinly sliced

Beat cream cheese in a bowl until smooth; gradually beat in sugar. Blend in sour cream and vanilla. Fold in whipped topping, blending well. Spread a thin layer of glaze over bottom of crust; layer strawberry slices on glaze. Cover with an additional layer of glaze; smooth cream cheese mixture on top. Cover and chill until set. Serves 8.

Vickie
Gooseberry Patch

No-Bake Strawberry
Cheesecake

Raspberry Truffle Cheesecake

Garnish with plump raspberries and sprigs of fresh mint…fabulous!

18 chocolate sandwich
   cookies, crushed
2 T. butter, melted
4 8-oz. pkgs. cream cheese,
   softened and divided
1¼ c. sugar
3 eggs

1 c. sour cream
1 t. almond extract
12-oz. pkg. semi-sweet
   chocolate chips, divided
⅓ c. raspberry preserves
¼ c. whipping cream

Combine cookie crumbs and butter in a bowl; press into the bottom of an ungreased 9" springform pan. Combine 3 packages cream cheese and sugar in a bowl; beat with an electric mixer at medium speed until blended. Add eggs, one at a time, beating well after each addition. Blend in sour cream and almond extract; pour over crust. Melt one cup chocolate chips in a saucepan over low heat. Remove from heat; stir in remaining cream cheese and preserves. Mix well and drop by rounded tablespoonfuls over plain cream cheese mixture. Bake at 325 degrees for one hour and 20 minutes. Cool; remove sides of pan. Melt remaining chocolate chips with whipping cream in a small saucepan over low heat, stirring until smooth. Spread over cheesecake, drizzling over sides. Chill 4 hours. Serves 12.

Deborah Hilton
Oswego, NY

easy slicing

When ready to serve, keep your knife in a glass of warm water. Warming the blade keeps the cheesecake from sticking.

Chewy Chocolate
Cookies, page 70

crunchy cookies + chewy bars

Pass the cookie jar! Frosted cookies, decadent brownies and rich bars fill this chapter with all the classics and some new favorites. Chock-full of our very best recipes...Molasses Sugar Cookies, Soft Gingerbread Cookies and Chewy Chocolate-Caramel Bars bake up in a jiffy.

Oatmeal-Raisin Spice Cookies

Easily made into a gift mix…just layer the first four ingredients in a wide-mouth, one-quart canning jar, packing down tightly in between each layer. Sift the next five ingredients and layer over oats. Attach a gift card with this recipe and baking directions.

¾ c. brown sugar, packed
½ c. sugar
¾ c. raisins
2 c. quick-cooking oats, uncooked
1 c. all-purpose flour
1 t. cinnamon

¼ t. nutmeg
1 t. baking powder
½ t. salt
¾ c. butter, softened
1 egg, beaten
1 t. vanilla extract

Combine dry ingredients in a large mixing bowl; add butter, egg and vanilla, mixing well. Shape into walnut-size balls; place on greased baking sheets. Bake at 350 degrees for 15 minutes, or until edges are golden brown. Cool on wire racks. Makes about 3 dozen.

Kim Robertson
South Hill, VA

Maple Drop Cookies

"Sometimes we top these with cream cheese frosting with a few drops of maple flavoring stirred in."

—Debi

1 c. butter, softened
¾ c. sugar
2 c. all-purpose flour

¼ t. salt
1½ t. maple flavoring
Optional: pecan halves

Blend butter and sugar in a bowl until light and fluffy; blend in remaining ingredients except pecan halves. Drop by teaspoonfuls onto greased baking sheets; place a pecan half on top of each cookie, if desired. Bake at 350 degrees for 12 to 15 minutes. Makes about 3 dozen.

Debi DeVore
Dover, OH

Oatmeal-Raisin
Spice Cookies

Molasses Sugar Cookies

¾ c. shortening
1 c. sugar
¼ c. molasses
1 egg
2 c. all-purpose flour
2 t. baking soda

1 t. cinnamon
½ t. ground cloves
½ t. ground ginger
½ t. salt
additional sugar

Melt shortening in a small saucepan over medium heat; pour into a large mixing bowl and cool. Add sugar, molasses and egg. Beat well. Sift together flour, baking soda, spices and salt in a separate bowl. Stir into molasses mixture. Chill 4 hours. Form into one-inch balls and roll in additional sugar. Place on greased baking sheets. Bake at 375 degrees for 8 to 10 minutes. Makes about 4 dozen.

Mary Sewell
Milford, CT

"When I bake these cookies, the smell reminds me of when my children were little. When they came home from school and realized I'd made them, they would jump for joy!"

—Mary

for the kiddos

Fill a white paper lunch bag with bite-size cookies or mini muffins. Fold the top over and trim with decorative-edge scissors. Tuck them inside the kids' school backpacks, and they'll find a sweet treat they can share!

Butterscotch
Cookies

Peanut Butter Cookies

Who doesn't love peanut butter and chocolate together? Here's a twist on a familiar cookie we think you'll love.

1 c. all-purpose flour
1 t. baking soda
⅛ t. salt
½ c. brown sugar, packed
¼ c. sugar
1 c. peanut butter

½ c. butter, softened
1 egg
½ t. vanilla extract
8-oz. pkg. chocolate star candies

Sift together flour, baking soda and salt in a small bowl. Blend sugars, peanut butter, butter, egg and vanilla in a large bowl. Stir dry ingredients into butter mixture until well blended. Refrigerate at least one hour. Roll into one-inch balls and bake at 375 degrees for 10 to 12 minutes. Remove from oven and place a chocolate star in the center of each cookie. Cool completely on a wire rack until chocolate sets. Makes about 2½ dozen.

Cindy Pogge
Kanawha, IA

Butterscotch Cookies

½ c. butter, softened
¾ c. sugar
¾ c. brown sugar, packed
2 eggs
1 t. vanilla extract
1½ c. all-purpose flour

1 t. salt
1 t. baking soda
12-oz. pkg. butterscotch chips
6-oz. pkg. toffee baking bits
1 c. chopped pecans

"A sure winner...this recipe won a ribbon at our county fair."

—Karen

Blend butter and sugars in a large bowl; add eggs and vanilla. Sift together flour, salt and baking soda in a separate bowl; stir into sugar mixture. Fold in chips, toffee bits and pecans; chill dough at least 30 minutes. Roll dough into 1½-inch balls; place on ungreased baking sheets at least 2 inches apart. Bake at 325 degrees for 9 to 12 minutes. Makes 5 to 6 dozen.

Karen Harris
Delaware, OH

White Chocolate-Cranberry Cookies

Dried cranberries have a surprisingly sweet taste…paired with white chocolate, they will make these cookies a new favorite.

¾ c. sugar
½ c. brown sugar, packed
1 c. sweetened dried cranberries
½ c. white chocolate chips
1¾ c. all-purpose flour
1 t. baking powder
½ t. baking soda
½ c. butter, softened
1 egg, beaten
1 t. vanilla extract

Combine sugars, cranberries, chips, flour, baking powder and baking soda in a large mixing bowl; blend in remaining ingredients. Shape into walnut-size balls; place on ungreased baking sheets 2 inches apart. Bake at 375 degrees for 12 to 15 minutes, until golden brown. Makes about 2½ dozen.

Shawna Brock
Eglin Air Force Base, FL

Honey + Spice Cookies

You can form the balls, then freeze if you're planning ahead. Just thaw, dip in sugar and bake.

4 c. brown sugar, packed
3 c. shortening
4 eggs
1 c. honey
9 c. all-purpose flour
2 T. baking soda
1 T. cinnamon
4 t. ground ginger
2 t. salt
1 t. ground cloves
sugar

Blend brown sugar and shortening in a large bowl; stir in eggs and honey. Stir in remaining ingredients except sugar and roll into balls. Dip into water and then roll in sugar. Bake at 350 degrees for 10 to 12 minutes. Makes 6 dozen.

Donna Fish
American Canyon, CA

White Chocolate-
Cranberry Cookies

Soft Gingerbread Cookies

1 c. margarine, softened
1½ c. brown sugar, packed
2 eggs, beaten
1 T. ground ginger
½ c. molasses
1½ c. boiling water

5 c. all-purpose flour
2 t. baking powder
1½ t. baking soda
1½ t. salt
1 T. cinnamon
1 c. chopped walnuts

Blend margarine and brown sugar in a large mixing bowl; blend in eggs. Mix in ginger and molasses; stir in boiling water. Set aside. Combine remaining ingredients except nuts in a separate bowl; add to sugar mixture. Fold in walnuts; cover and refrigerate dough at least 2 hours. Drop by teaspoonfuls onto ungreased baking sheets; bake at 425 degrees for 10 to 12 minutes. Makes about 6 dozen.

Bev Johnstone
Delaware, OH

"My mother always made these cookies at Christmastime when I was a little girl. I carried on the tradition for my children and now make them for my grandson. They are so soft and moist... a true favorite."

—Bev

in a snip

A quick and easy cookie decorating tip: Add chocolate, peanut butter or raspberry chips to a plastic zipping bag, seal and microwave until chips are melted. Then just snip off one small corner and pipe designs onto cooled cookies.

Oatmeal Crinkles

"So delicious, my husband can't wait for them to cool...he eats them as soon as they come out of the oven."

—Krista

1¼ c. sugar, divided
1 t. cinnamon
1 c. shortening
1 c. brown sugar, packed
2 eggs
1 t. vanilla extract
1 t. almond extract

2 c. all-purpose flour
1 t. baking powder
1 t. baking soda
1 t. salt
2½ c. long-cooking oats, uncooked
1½ c. raisins

Combine ¼ cup sugar and cinnamon in a small bowl; set aside. Blend shortening, remaining sugar, brown sugar, eggs and extracts in a large mixing bowl; set aside. Combine remaining ingredients in a separate bowl; stir well. Add to sugar mixture; mix well. Roll into walnut-size balls; roll in sugar and cinnamon mixture. Place on ungreased baking sheets 2 inches apart; bake at 350 degrees for 10 minutes. Cool on baking sheets 2 minutes; remove to cool on wire racks. Makes about 5 dozen.

Krista Starnes
Beaufort, SC

Chewy Chocolate Cookies

Add chocolate chips for a richer cookie!

½ c. shortening
1⅔ c. sugar
2 eggs
2 t. vanilla extract
5 T. baking cocoa

2 c. all-purpose flour
2 t. baking powder
½ t. salt
⅓ c. milk
½ c. nuts, chopped

Blend shortening and sugar in a large bowl. Add eggs and vanilla; stir in cocoa. Sift together flour, baking powder and salt in a separate bowl; add to cocoa mixture alternately with milk. Stir in nuts. Drop by spoonfuls on ungreased baking sheets. Bake at 350 degrees for 8 to 10 minutes. Makes about 2 dozen.

Margaret Scoresby
Mount Vernon, OH

Chocolate Thumbprint Cookies

A chocolatey twist to an old favorite.

½ c. plus 1 t. butter, softened
  and divided
1 c. sugar, divided
1 egg yolk
2 T. plus 2 t. milk, divided
2¼ t. vanilla extract, divided

1 c. all-purpose flour
⅓ c. baking cocoa
¼ t. salt
½ c. powdered sugar
24 milk chocolate drops

Beat ½ cup butter, ⅔ cup sugar, egg yolk, 2 tablespoons milk and 2 teaspoons vanilla in a large bowl until light and fluffy; set aside. Combine flour, cocoa and salt in a separate bowl; add to butter mixture, beating until well blended. Refrigerate dough at least one hour; shape into one-inch balls. Roll in remaining sugar; place on lightly greased baking sheets. Press thumb gently into center of each ball; bake at 350 degrees for 10 to 12 minutes. Stir together powdered sugar, remaining butter, milk and vanilla in a small bowl. Spoon ¼ teaspoon filling into each thumbprint; gently press chocolate drop on top of filling. Remove from baking sheets to a wire rack and cool completely. Makes 2 dozen.

Ann Fehr
Trappe, PA

Snickerdoodles

An old-fashioned favorite that no one will pass up!

kitchen tip

Use the bottom of a juice glass to flatten these cookies.

1¼ c. butter, softened
2½ c. sugar, divided
2 eggs
1½ t. vanilla extract
½ t. lemon extract
4½ c. all-purpose flour

2 t. baking powder
1 t. baking soda
¾ t. salt
1 c. buttermilk
2 T. cinnamon

Blend butter and 2 cups sugar in a large bowl; add eggs, one at a time, mixing well after each addition. Blend in extracts; set aside. Combine flour, baking powder, baking soda and salt in a separate bowl; add alternately with buttermilk to sugar mixture. Cover and chill dough 4 hours; shape ¼-cup measure of dough into balls. Mix remaining sugar and cinnamon in a small bowl. Roll balls in sugar and cinnamon mixture; gently press balls to ½-inch thickness. Place 5 or 6 on each ungreased baking sheet; bake at 375 degrees for 15 minutes. Makes about 3 dozen.

Dolores Berg
Selah, WA

No-Bake Cookies

No get-together is complete without these all-time favorites!

½ c. butter
2 c. sugar
⅓ c. baking cocoa
¼ t. salt
½ c. milk

¾ c. creamy peanut butter
3 c. quick-cooking oats, uncooked
1 t. vanilla extract

Combine butter, sugar, cocoa, salt and milk in a saucepan over medium heat and bring to a boil; boil one to 2 minutes, stirring constantly. Remove from heat; stir in remaining ingredients. Drop by tablespoonfuls onto wax paper; cool. Makes about 4 dozen.

Chocolate Chip-Raisin Cookies

1 c. margarine, softened
1 c. shortening
2 c. sugar
2 c. brown sugar, packed
2 t. vanilla extract
4 eggs
4 c. all-purpose flour

2 t. baking soda
2 t. salt
3½ c. quick-cooking oats
2 c. walnuts, chopped
2 c. chocolate chips
2 c. raisins

"Sometimes I add extra chocolate chips instead of raisins, or you could use peanut butter or butterscotch chips."

—Judy

Blend margarine, shortening, sugars and vanilla in a large bowl. Add eggs, blending well. Stir in dry ingredients just until blended. Add nuts, chocolate chips and raisins. Drop by spoonfuls on ungreased baking sheets and bake at 375 degrees for 12 to 14 minutes, until golden. Makes about 6 dozen.

Judy Borecky
Escondido, CA

Peanut Butter Jumbos
Julie Anthony (Homeworth, OH)

Everyone loves peanut butter and chocolate!

¼ c. butter, softened
1 c. brown sugar, packed
1 c. sugar
1½ c. creamy peanut butter
3 eggs
2 t. baking soda

1 t. vanilla extract
4½ c. quick-cooking oats, uncooked
1 c. chocolate chips
1 c. candy-coated chocolate mini
baking bits

Blend butter, sugars, peanut butter and eggs in a large mixing bowl; blend in baking soda, vanilla and oats. Fold in chocolate chips and mini baking bits; drop by tablespoonfuls onto greased baking sheets. Bake at 350 degrees for 15 to 20 minutes. Makes about 1½ dozen.

Old-Fashioned Raspberry Cut-Outs

1 c. butter, room temperature
½ c. sugar
1 c. walnuts

2 c. all-purpose flour
additional sugar
raspberry jam

Blend butter and sugar in a large bowl. Chop walnuts in a food processor or blend to nearly a paste consistency. Blend flour and chopped walnuts into butter mixture. Roll out onto a floured surface and cut into your favorite shapes. Place on ungreased baking sheets. Bake at 350 degrees for 10 minutes. Be careful not to overbake; cookies should be soft. While cookies are still warm, roll in sugar and fill with jam, pressing 2 cookies gently together. Makes 2 to 3 dozen, depending on size of cookie cutter.

Rebecca LaDue
Oshkosh, WI

"These cookies represent many happy memories of special occasions. The recipe is over 90 years old, given to my mother by an elderly neighbor who was like a grandmother to me."

—Rebecca

Frosted Orange Cookies

2 navel oranges
½ c. butter-flavored shortening
1 c. sugar
½ c. milk
2 c. all-purpose flour

1 t. baking powder
½ t. baking soda
½ t. salt
2½ c. powdered sugar
1 t. butter, melted

Score each orange into quarters; peel. Quarter oranges; add to a blender with peels. Blend until smooth; measure out ¾ cup, refrigerating any remaining orange mixture for another use. Blend shortening and sugar in a large mixing bowl; blend in milk and 6 tablespoons orange mixture. Set aside. Combine flour, baking powder, baking soda and salt in a separate bowl; stir into sugar mixture. Drop by teaspoonfuls on greased baking sheets 2 inches apart; bake at 350 degrees for 10 to 13 minutes. Remove to wire racks to cool completely. Whisk together powdered sugar, butter and enough of the remaining orange mixture in a bowl to a desired spreading consistency; frost cookies. Makes about 4 dozen.

DarLinda Adams
Orlando, FL

Polka-Dot Cookies

Try different combinations for these cookies…white chocolate or peanut butter chips, cashews or macadamia nuts.

½ c. butter or margarine
½ c. sugar
½ c. brown sugar, packed
1 egg
1 t. vanilla extract
2 c. all-purpose flour
1 t. baking powder

½ t. salt
¼ t. baking soda
¼ c. milk
6-oz. pkg. chocolate chips
½ c. maraschino cherries, chopped
½ c. chopped pecans

Blend butter or margarine and sugars in a large bowl; blend in egg and vanilla. Sift together flour, baking powder, salt and baking soda in a separate mixing bowl; add alternating with milk to the sugar mixture. Stir in chocolate chips, cherries and pecans; drop by tablespoonfuls onto a greased baking sheet. Bake at 350 degrees for 10 minutes. Makes 2 dozen.

Amy Blanchard
Ocean City, NJ

Frosted Sugar Cookies

2 c. butter, softened
1⅓ c. sugar
2 eggs, beaten
2 t. vanilla extract
5 c. all-purpose flour
Garnish: colored sugar

Blend butter and sugar in a large bowl; stir in eggs and vanilla. Add flour; mix until well blended. Shape into a ball; cover and chill 4 hours to overnight. Roll out dough ¼-inch thick on a lightly floured surface; cut out with cookie cutters as desired. Arrange cookies on lightly greased baking sheets. Bake at 350 degrees for 8 to 10 minutes, until golden. Spread Frosting on cooled cookies; decorate as desired. Makes 4 dozen.

Frosting

4½ c. powdered sugar
6 T. butter, melted
6 T. milk
2 T. vanilla extract
1 T. lemon juice
Optional: food coloring

Combine all ingredients in a medium bowl. Beat with an electric mixer at low speed until smooth.

June Lemen
Nashua, NH

"We love to bake cut-out cookies year 'round for holidays... you can't beat this recipe!"

—June

colorful idea

Let kids decorate cookies with edible cookie paint! You'll need one egg yolk for each color of "paint." Drop egg yolks into separate bowls, stir with fork and add ¼ teaspoon of a different food coloring to each yolk; mix well. Brush paint on cookies and then bake according to recipe.

Gumdrop Cookies

"These are special to me because my mother always made them on my first day of school."

—Karen

1 c. shortening
1 c. sugar
1 c. brown sugar, packed
4 eggs, beaten
1 c. gumdrops

2 c. quick-cooking oats, uncooked
1 t. baking powder
1 t. baking soda
2¼ c. all-purpose flour

Blend shortening, sugars and eggs in a large mixing bowl; stir in gumdrops. Combine oats, baking powder, baking soda and flour in a separate bowl; blend into sugar mixture. Drop by teaspoonfuls onto greased baking sheets. Bake at 350 degrees for 10 to 15 minutes, until done. Makes 4 dozen.

Karen Moran
Navasota, TX

spooktacular idea

Use any leftover Halloween candy as fun mix-in ideas for cookies.

Old-Time Icebox Cookies

1 c. butter or margarine	1 t. baking soda
2 c. brown sugar, packed	½ t. salt
2 eggs	1 c. chopped nuts
3½ c. all-purpose flour	

Blend butter and sugar in a large mixing bowl. Add eggs, one at a time, beating well after each addition. Combine flour, baking soda and salt in a separate bowl; add to sugar mixture, mixing well. Fold in nuts; divide dough and roll into 2 logs. Wrap in wax paper; refrigerate overnight. Slice thinly and place on greased baking sheets; bake at 350 degrees for 7 to 10 minutes. Makes 4 dozen.

Rosalie Benson
Coats, NC

"As a child, it was my job to empty the drip pan beneath the icebox each night... sometimes I forgot. If we heard grumbling when my father arose in the morning, I knew he'd stepped in overflowing water on the kitchen floor!"

—Rosalie

Melt-in-Your-Mouth Cookies

True to their name, these cookies really do melt in your mouth!

1 c. butter, softened	¾ c. cornstarch
5½ T. powdered sugar	1 c. all-purpose flour

Blend butter, powdered sugar and cornstarch in a bowl. Add flour and mix well. Roll into balls or drop by teaspoonfuls onto a greased baking sheet. Bake at 350 degrees for 20 minutes. Spread Glaze over cooled cookies. Makes 3 dozen.

Glaze

¾ c. powdered sugar	milk
½ t. banana flavoring	yellow food coloring

Mix powdered sugar, flavoring and just enough milk to make glaze spreadable in a bowl. Add coloring to desired shade; mix well.

Bethany Zemaitis
Pittsburgh, PA

Clothespin Cookies

Tint the filling any color. Pastels are really pretty…or just dip the ends of the cookies in colored sugar.

1 lb. butter, softened
24-oz. container small-curd
  cottage cheese
½ t. salt

4 c. all-purpose flour
30 to 60 rounded clothespins
Garnish: powdered sugar

Combine butter, cottage cheese and salt in a large mixing bowl and mix well. Add flour in ½-cup increments until incorporated; dough will be thick and sticky. Using an equal mixture of sugar and flour on the rolling surface, divide dough into 4 equal parts; roll out each part into a rectangle ⅛-inch thick. Cut dough into 5"x2" rectangles, then diagonally cut each rectangle to form 2 triangles. Roll each triangle around a dry clothespin, wide end first, to form a crescent-like roll. Lay on a lightly greased baking sheet with point of crescent facing up. Dough will not spread; do not let crescents touch. Bake at 350 degrees for 15 to 20 minutes, until dough is set and bottoms of cookies are light brown. Slide off clothespins while cookies are still warm. Cool and fill with Cream Filling. Dust with powdered sugar before serving. Makes 12 to 14 dozen.

Cream Filling

4 t. meringue powder
¼ c. water
1 c. butter, softened
1 c. shortening

2 t. vanilla extract
4 c. powdered sugar
1 c. half-and-half, warmed

Blend meringue powder and water in a large bowl; add butter, shortening and vanilla, blending well. Add powdered sugar slowly, mixing well until smooth. Pour in half-and-half; beat 5 to 8 minutes, until very creamy and light. Use a pastry bag to pipe filling into cooled shells.

Gloria Mulhern
Windham, OH

Hucklebucks

¾ c. shortening
2 eggs
¾ c. baking cocoa
1 T. vanilla extract, divided
1½ c. sugar
3 c. all-purpose flour

1 T. baking powder
¾ t. plus ⅛ t. salt, divided
1½ c. plus 1 T. milk, divided
¾ c. butter, softened
2 c. powdered sugar
1 c. marshmallow creme

Blend shortening, eggs, cocoa, 1½ teaspoons vanilla and sugar in a large bowl. Sift together flour, baking powder and ¾ teaspoon salt in a separate bowl. Alternately add flour mixture and 1½ cups milk to cocoa mixture, mixing well after each addition until batter is smooth. Drop by tablespoonfuls onto ungreased baking sheets. Bake at 400 degrees for 7 to 8 minutes; cool. Blend butter, powdered sugar, marshmallow creme, remaining vanilla, salt and milk in a bowl; spread filling on flat bottom side of one cookie and top with a second cookie, bottom-side down. Repeat with remaining cookies and filling; store in an airtight container. Makes 1½ dozen.

Shannon Ellis
Mount Vernon, WA

Spritz

Give spritz cookies a new twist. Shape the dough into rings and decorate with sprinkles…sweet wreaths to hang on a Christmas tree!

1 c. butter, softened
½ c. sugar
1 egg yolk
½ t. almond extract
2 c. all-purpose flour
¼ t. salt

Blend butter and sugar in a large bowl; add egg yolk and almond extract. Sift together flour and salt in a separate bowl; add to sugar mixture. Press dough through a cookie press, using a small star disk, and shape into letters of the alphabet on ungreased baking sheets. Bake at 350 degrees for 8 to 10 minutes, until golden. Makes 5 to 6 dozen.

Juanita Williams
Jacksonville, OR

"Many, many good memories come with this recipe. Taken from one of Mom's old Swedish cookbooks, it makes great cookies every time."

—Juanita

Thumbprint Cookies

Fill these yummy cookies with your favorite flavor of jam or jelly!

½ c. butter, softened
3 T. powdered sugar
1 t. vanilla extract
1 c. all-purpose flour
1 c. nuts, finely chopped
8-oz. jar strawberry jelly
Garnish: powdered sugar

Blend butter and sugar in a large bowl; stir in vanilla. Add flour and nuts a little at a time until mixed; chill overnight. Roll dough into equal-size balls and arrange on an ungreased baking sheet. Place thumb in the middle of each ball, flattening slightly, and fill with jelly. Bake at 375 degrees for 15 minutes, or until golden. Sprinkle cooled cookies with powdered sugar. Makes one dozen.

Calico Inn
Sevierville, TN

Rocky Road Treats

If you love rocky road ice cream, try these chocolatey squares.

½ c. butter, melted
1 c. sugar
⅓ c. baking cocoa
2 eggs
2 t. vanilla extract

1 c. all-purpose flour
½ t. baking powder
⅓ c. chopped pecans
Garnish: chopped pecans and
   toffee baking bits

Whisk together butter, sugar, cocoa, eggs and vanilla in a bowl; add flour and baking powder. Fold in pecans; spread in a greased aluminum foil-lined 9"x9" baking pan. Bake at 350 degrees for 20 minutes; cool. Pour Icing over the top; cool. Sprinkle with garnishes; cut into bars. Serves 8.

Icing

3 T. butter
½ c. powdered sugar
1 c. mini marshmallows

2 T. baking cocoa
2 T. milk

Combine all ingredients in a heavy saucepan; heat over medium-low heat. Stir until marshmallows melt and mixture is smooth.

Tina Wright
Atlanta, GA

tasty twist

For over-the-top decadence, crumble these treats over vanilla ice cream.

gift-giving idea

Give these delicious treats away in style. Simple shipping tags can become gift tags in a snap…just glue on a vintage sticker, buttons or a family photo!

Whoopie Pies

2¼ c. plus 5 t. all-purpose flour, divided
½ c. baking cocoa
1½ t. baking soda
1¼ c. sugar
1¼ t. cream of tartar
1⅔ c. shortening, divided
2 c. milk, divided
2 eggs
1 T. plus 1 t. vanilla extract, divided
½ c. butter, softened
1 c. powdered sugar
¼ t. salt

Mix together 2¼ cups flour, cocoa, baking soda, sugar, cream of tartar, ⅔ cup shortening, one cup milk, eggs and one teaspoon vanilla in a large bowl. Drop by teaspoonfuls onto greased baking sheets. Bake at 300 degrees for 15 minutes. Cook remaining milk and flour in a saucepan over medium heat until thick; cool. Stir in remaining one cup shortening, remaining one tablespoon vanilla, butter, powdered sugar and salt; beat until fluffy. Spread filling between 2 cooled cookies; repeat with remaining filling and cookies. Wrap in plastic wrap; chill. Makes 2 dozen.

Karen Slack
Mount Pleasant, TX

"When I was a school secretary, a student always brought these to me, and they quickly became a favorite."

—Karen

Crème de Menthe Cookies

This is the perfect combination of mint and chocolate…all wrapped up in a soft, chewy cookie!

¾ c. butter
1½ c. brown sugar, packed
2 T. water
2 c. chocolate chips
2 eggs

2½ c. all-purpose flour
1¼ t. baking soda
3 4.67-oz. boxes crème de
  menthe thins, unwrapped
  and halved

Heat butter, brown sugar and water in a saucepan over medium heat until sugar is dissolved; remove from heat. Stir in chocolate chips until melted; cool 10 minutes. Blend in eggs; set aside. Combine flour and baking soda in a bowl; add to chocolate mixture, mixing well. Cover with plastic wrap; chill one hour. Roll dough into walnut-size balls; bake on ungreased baking sheets at 350 degrees for 8 to 9 minutes. Remove from oven and immediately place a mint wafer half on top of each ball. Spread like frosting when melted. Makes 3 dozen.

Jennifer Canfield
Davenport, IA

Honey-Pecan Bars

Chock-full of things that are not only good, but good for you!

1½ c. sesame seeds
1 c. flaked coconut
½ c. sunflower seeds
½ c. chopped pecans

¾ c. honey
¼ c. powdered milk
½ t. vanilla extract

Toast sesame seeds, coconut, sunflower seeds and pecans in an ungreased 11"x8" baking pan at 400 degrees for about 20 minutes; stir occasionally. Combine honey and powdered milk in a saucepan; bring to a boil. Remove from heat; add vanilla. Pour honey mixture over seeds; stir well and press together. Allow to cool; cut into bars and wrap individually in plastic wrap. Makes 1½ dozen.

Jackie Crough
Salina, KS

make-ahead magic

Make these yummy bars up to 3 days ahead.

Chewy Chocolate-Caramel Bars

These chewy bars will be a hit at any bake sale!

tasty twist

Substitute dark chocolate chips for a richer flavor.

1 c. quick-cooking oats, uncooked
½ c. brown sugar, packed
½ c. sugar
1 c. all-purpose flour
1 t. baking soda
¾ c. butter, melted
14-oz. pkg. caramels, unwrapped
3 T. milk
12-oz. pkg. milk chocolate chips

Combine oats, brown sugar, sugar, flour, baking soda and butter in a bowl; press half of mixture into a greased 9"x9" baking pan. Bake at 350 degrees for 10 minutes. Melt caramel with milk in a double boiler over medium heat; stir until smooth. Sprinkle chocolate chips over hot crust; pour melted caramel on top. Spread remaining dry mixture over top; bake 15 more minutes. Cool; cut into bars. Makes one dozen.

Linda Kohrs
Mesa, AZ

welcoming idea

Say "welcome" to new co-workers…leave a basket of candy, cookies or brownies on their desk. If they're new to town, be sure to include directions to all the best places for lunch, the bank and the post office.

Coffee-Toffee Bars

Just the right size to nibble on.

2½ c. all-purpose flour
½ t. baking powder
½ t. salt
1 c. butter, softened
1 c. brown sugar, packed

1 t. almond extract
2 T. instant coffee granules
½ c. chopped pecans
6-oz. pkg. chocolate chips

Combine all ingredients in a large bowl; mix well. Press into a greased 13"x9" baking pan; bake at 350 degrees for 20 to 25 minutes. Cool; spread with Frosting. Cut into bars. Makes about 2 dozen.

Frosting

1 T. butter, softened
¾ c. powdered sugar

⅛ t. almond extract
1 T. water

Blend ingredients in a small bowl until smooth and creamy, adjusting amount of water for desired spreading consistency.

Valerie Hugus
Circleville, OH

Raspberry-Coconut Bars

1⅔ c. graham cracker crumbs
½ c. butter, melted
7-oz. pkg. flaked coconut
14-oz. can sweetened
   condensed milk

1 c. raspberry jam
⅓ c. chopped nuts
½ c. chocolate chips, melted
½ c. white chocolate chips,
   melted

Mix crumbs and butter in a bowl; press into a greased 13"x9" baking pan. Sprinkle with coconut; pour milk over the top. Bake at 350 degrees for 20 minutes; cool. Spread with raspberry jam; refrigerate 3 to 4 hours. Sprinkle with nuts; drizzle with melted chocolates. Chill until serving time; cut into small bars. Makes 2 dozen.

Roberta Lind
APO, England

tasty twist

If you really like raspberries, try raspberry chips instead of white chocolate...either way, these won't last long.

Banana Bars

Enjoy these as they are, or frost with a buttercream frosting and drizzle with chocolate syrup...delicious!

½ c. butter, softened
1½ c. sugar
2 eggs, beaten
1 c. bananas, mashed
1 t. vanilla extract

2 c. all-purpose flour
½ t. salt
1 t. baking soda
¾ c. buttermilk

Blend butter and sugar in a large bowl; add eggs. Mix in bananas, vanilla, flour, salt and baking soda; gradually blend in buttermilk. Spread in a greased 15"x10" jelly-roll pan; bake at 350 degrees for 15 to 20 minutes. Cool; cut into bars. Makes 3 dozen.

Romola Knotts
Woodstock, OH

Grandmother's Oatmeal Bars

Topped with a tasty chocolate and peanut butter icing!

4 c. **quick-cooking oats**
½ c. **corn syrup**
2 t. **vanilla extract**
1 c. **brown sugar**, packed

⅔ c. **butter**, melted
12-oz. pkg. **chocolate chips**
⅔ c. **peanut butter**

Mix oats, corn syrup, vanilla, brown sugar and butter in a large bowl. Place in a lightly oiled 13"x9" baking pan. Bake at 350 degrees for 10 to 15 minutes. Melt chocolate chips and peanut butter in a small saucepan over medium-low heat; spread on cooled bars. Makes about 3 dozen.

Dixie Sorensen
Exira, IA

Peanut Butter Bars
Angela Sims (Willow Springs, IL)

Make a good thing even better…drizzle with melted chocolate. Yum!

1½ c. graham cracker crumbs
1 c. margarine, melted
16-oz. pkg. powdered sugar

1 c. creamy peanut butter
12-oz. pkg. butterscotch chips

Combine graham cracker crumbs, margarine, powdered sugar and peanut butter in a bowl; mix well. Press into the bottom of a lightly greased 13"x9" baking pan; set aside. Melt butterscotch chips in a double boiler over medium heat; spread over crumb mixture. Refrigerate several hours to overnight, until firm. Cut into bars. Makes 2 dozen.

Fudgy Oatmeal Bars

2 c. brown sugar, packed
1 c. plus 2 T. margarine,
  softened and divided
2 t. vanilla extract, divided
2 eggs
2½ c. all-purpose flour
1 t. baking soda

1 t. salt, divided
3 c. quick-cooking oats
14-oz. can sweetened
  condensed milk
12-oz. pkg. chocolate chips
1 c. walnuts, chopped

"I like to tuck these into my daughters' lunchboxes."

—Becky

Mix brown sugar, one cup margarine, one teaspoon vanilla and eggs in a large bowl. Sift together flour, baking soda and ½ teaspoon salt in a separate bowl; stir in oats and add to egg mixture. Reserve one-third of the oat mixture; press remaining oat mixture into a greased 15"x10" jelly-roll pan. Heat remaining 2 tablespoons margarine, condensed milk and chocolate chips in a saucepan over low heat, stirring constantly, until chocolate is melted; remove from heat. Stir in nuts, remaining vanilla and salt. Spread over oat mixture in pan. Drop reserved oat mixture by rounded teaspoonfuls onto chocolate mixture. Bake at 350 degrees for 25 to 30 minutes, until golden brown. Cut into bars while warm. Makes about 3 dozen.

Becky Sykes
Gooseberry Patch

Sour Cream-Apple Squares

Just like apple pie!

2 c. all-purpose flour
2 c. brown sugar, packed
½ c. margarine, softened
½ c. nuts, chopped
2 t. cinnamon
1 t. baking soda
½ t. salt

1 c. sour cream
1 t. vanilla extract
1 egg, beaten
2 c. apples, peeled, cored and
    chopped
Garnish: whipped cream

Combine flour, brown sugar and margarine in a large bowl; beat with an electric mixer at low speed until crumbly. Stir in nuts. Press about 2¾ cups crumb mixture into the bottom of an ungreased 13"x9" baking pan. Add cinnamon, baking soda, salt, sour cream, vanilla and egg to remaining crumb mixture. Beat until thoroughly combined. Stir in apples. Spoon evenly over bottom layer. Bake at 350 degrees for 35 to 40 minutes. Cool in pan on a wire rack. Cut into squares. Garnish with whipped cream. Makes 12 to 15.

Pat Habiger
Spearville, KS

à la mode

Top these fall-inspired squares with vanilla ice cream.

Chocolate-Butter Cream Squares

Tastes like a combination of brownies and butter cream candy.

¼ c. butter, softened
½ c. sugar
1 egg, beaten
1-oz. sq. unsweetened baking
   chocolate, melted

½ c. all-purpose flour
¼ c. chopped nuts

Blend butter, sugar and egg in a bowl; stir in chocolate, flour and nuts. Spread evenly in a greased and floured 8"x8" baking pan; bake at 350 degrees for 10 minutes. Cool; spread with Filling and then Icing over the top. Chill until set; cut into small squares. Makes 2 dozen.

Filling

2 T. margarine, softened
1 c. powdered sugar

1 T. whipping cream
½ t. vanilla extract

Blend all ingredients in a small bowl until smooth and creamy. Refrigerate 10 minutes before spreading.

Icing

1-oz. sq. unsweetened baking
   chocolate

1 T. butter or margarine

Melt ingredients together in a double boiler over medium heat; stir until blended.

Dorothy Armijo
Dallas, TX

kitchen tip

For sticky ingredients, spray spatulas with nonstick vegetable spray for easy spreading.

Fudgy-Topped Brownies

These truly satisfy a chocolate craving!

½ c. butter, softened
1 c. sugar
4 eggs, beaten
1 c. all-purpose flour

16-oz. can chocolate syrup
1 t. vanilla extract
1 c. chopped nuts

Blend butter and sugar in a bowl. Stir in eggs, flour, chocolate syrup, vanilla and nuts. Bake at 350 degrees in a greased 13"x9" baking pan for 40 minutes or in a greased 15"x10" jelly-roll pan for 20 minutes. Spread Frosting over warm brownies. Cut into bars. Makes 2 dozen.

Frosting

1⅓ c. sugar
6 T. butter

6 T. milk
6-oz. pkg. chocolate chips

Combine sugar, butter and milk in a saucepan over medium heat; stir until completely dissolved. Bring to a boil for one minute. Remove from heat and add chocolate chips. Mix quickly until chips dissolve.

Carole Foltman
Williams Bay, WI

sharing is caring

Hosting a family reunion? Bake bite-size desserts to share...cupcakes, brownies and cookies are easy to snack on while everyone spends time catching up.

Birthday Brownies

Caramel Brownies

A great after-school treat with a glass of icy-cold cider!

14-oz. pkg. caramels, unwrapped
⅔ c. evaporated milk, divided
18¼-oz. pkg. German chocolate cake mix
⅔ c. butter, softened
1 c. pecans, chopped
12-oz. pkg. chocolate chips

Combine caramels and ⅓ cup evaporated milk in a microwave-safe bowl. Microwave, stirring occasionally, until caramels have melted. Combine cake mix with remaining ⅓ cup milk and butter in a bowl. Press half of mixture in a greased and floured 13"x9" baking pan and bake at 350 degrees for 8 minutes. Remove from oven. Scatter chopped pecans and chocolate chips over crust, then drizzle caramel mixture over chips. Drop remaining cake mixture by spoonfuls on top of caramels and bake 18 minutes. Let cool before cutting. Makes 2 dozen.

Jody Komarnitzki
Venice, FL

Birthday Brownies

¾ c. margarine, softened
1¼ c. sugar
1¼ c. brown sugar, packed
3 eggs
2½ t. baking powder
½ t. salt
1 t. vanilla extract
2¼ c. all-purpose flour
12-oz. pkg. chocolate chips

Blend margarine and sugars in a large bowl until very smooth. Add eggs, baking powder, salt and vanilla. Mix in flour; stir in chocolate chips and spread in a buttered 13"x9" baking pan. Bake at 400 degrees for 20 minutes, or until a toothpick inserted in the center comes out clean. Makes 16 large brownies.

Mary Ann Clark
Indian Springs, OH

"My children often request these quick and easy brownies as treats for their birthdays."
—Mary Ann

Chocolate-Raspberry Brownies

The raspberry layer makes these brownies really special.

1 c. unsalted butter
5 1-oz. sqs. unsweetened chocolate, chopped
2 c. sugar
4 eggs
2 t. vanilla extract

1¼ c. all-purpose flour
1 t. baking powder
½ t. salt
1 c. walnuts, toasted and chopped
½ c. raspberry preserves

Melt butter and chocolate in a heavy saucepan over low heat, stirring constantly until smooth. Remove from heat. Whisk in sugar, eggs and vanilla. Mix flour, baking powder and salt in a small bowl. Add to chocolate mixture and whisk to blend. Stir in nuts. Pour 2 cups batter into a buttered 13"x9" baking pan. Freeze until firm, about 10 minutes. Spread preserves over frozen brownie batter in pan; spoon remaining batter over preserves. Let stand 20 minutes at room temperature to thaw. Bake at 350 degrees for 35 minutes, or until a toothpick inserted in the center comes out clean. Cool in pan on a wire rack. Cut into squares. Makes about 2 dozen.

Susan Brzozowski
Ellicott City, MD

Cappuccino Brownies

If you love the blend of coffee and chocolate, give these a try!

4 1-oz. sqs. **unsweetened chocolate,** melted
¾ c. **butter,** melted
2⅓ c. **sugar,** divided
5 **eggs,** divided
1 t. **vanilla extract**

3 T. **instant coffee granules**
1¼ c. plus 2 T. **all-purpose flour,** divided
8-oz. pkg. **cream cheese,** softened
½ t. **cinnamon**

Place chocolate and butter in a large bowl; stir in 2 cups sugar until well blended. Mix in 4 eggs, vanilla and coffee. Stir in 1¼ cups flour until combined. Spread in a greased aluminum foil-lined 13"x9" baking pan. Beat cream cheese, remaining ⅓ cup sugar, remaining egg, remaining 2 tablespoons flour and cinnamon in a bowl until well blended. Spoon mixture over brownie batter and swirl with a knife to marble top. Bake at 350 degrees for 40 minutes, or until a toothpick inserted in the center comes out with fudgy crumbs. Cool in pan on a wire rack. Cut into squares. Makes 2 dozen.

Robin Paterson
Roseburg, OR

cookie swap

Having a cookie exchange? Display your cookies in creative ways...on tiered cake stands, tucked into painted clay pots, dough bowls, vintage cookie jars, nostalgic hatboxes, painted tins or layered in a tall glass trifle bowl.

Grandma's Easy
Peach Cobbler,
page 129

old-fashioned pies, cobblers + tarts

Warm and juicy from the oven or cream-filled and frosty from the fridge, pies are everyone's favorite dessert. Enjoy homemade favorites like Peanut Butter Strudel Pie, Autumn Apple Pie, Blackberry Cobbler and Glazed Strawberry Tart.

Fudge Brownie Pie

"Just as good now as back in 1914, when it first appeared in a YMCA cookbook."

—Flo

1 c. sugar
½ c. margarine, melted
2 eggs, beaten
½ c. all-purpose flour
⅓ c. baking cocoa

¼ t. salt
2 t. vanilla extract
½ c. chopped walnuts
Garnish: whipped cream

Beat sugar and margarine in a bowl. Add eggs; mix well. Stir in flour, cocoa and salt; mix in vanilla and nuts. Pour into a greased and floured 9" pie plate; bake at 350 degrees for 25 to 30 minutes. Cut into wedges; top with dollops of whipped cream. Serves 6 to 8.

Flo Burtnett
Gage, OK

German Chocolate Pie

A quick and easy recipe for family gatherings.

2 1-oz. sqs. German sweet
   chocolate
1 c. butter
3 eggs
2 T. all-purpose flour
1 c. sugar

1 t. vanilla extract
1 c. pecans, chopped
½ c. flaked coconut
Garnish: whipped cream,
   shaved chocolate and
   chopped pecans

Melt chocolate and butter in a saucepan over low heat; let cool. Beat eggs, flour, sugar and vanilla in a bowl with an electric mixer at high speed 3 minutes. Pour chocolate mixture over egg mixture and beat 3 more minutes. Add pecans and coconut. Pour into a well-buttered 9" pie plate. Bake at 350 degrees for 28 minutes. Cool before serving. Top with whipped cream and garnish with shaved chocolate and pecans. Serves 6.

Pauline Raens
Abilene, TX

Chocolate-Butterscotch Pie

This classic is a favorite from the 1930s.

¾ c. brown sugar, packed
⅓ c. all-purpose flour
½ t. salt
2½ c. milk
6 T. chocolate syrup

2 egg yolks, beaten
2 T. butter
½ t. vanilla extract
9-inch pie crust, baked
Garnish: whipped topping

Thoroughly combine brown sugar, flour and salt in a saucepan; stir in milk, chocolate syrup and egg yolks. Cook over medium heat until thick, stirring constantly. Remove from heat; blend in butter and vanilla. Pour into pie crust; cool to room temperature. Refrigerate until firm; spread whipped topping over top. Serves 8.

Kathy Grashoff
Fort Wayne, IN

Maple-Walnut Pie

"After an afternoon spent raking leaves, jumping in them and raking them again, we love to come inside and enjoy a slice of this pie."

—Lynda

4 eggs, beaten
1½ c. maple syrup
2 T. all-purpose flour
3 T. butter, melted and cooled
2 t. vanilla extract

¾ c. walnuts, chopped
9-inch pie crust
Optional: whipped cream and crushed walnuts

Combine eggs and maple syrup in a large bowl. Beat in flour, butter and vanilla until well blended. Fold in walnuts and pour into pie crust. Bake at 375 degrees for 35 minutes; pie filling will be soft when baked. Top with whipped cream and crushed nuts, if desired. Serves 8.

Lynda Robson
Boston, MA

Apple-Dapple Pie

Serve slices warm with a spoonful of whipped cream and a sprinkle of nutmeg on top.

2 T. crushed pineapple
14½-oz. can cherry pie filling
2 c. apples, peeled, cored and sliced
2 T. tapioca
1 T. cornstarch

¾ c. sugar
¼ t. cinnamon
⅛ t. nutmeg
1 t. butter, softened
9-inch pie crust

Combine pineapple, cherry pie filling and apples in a large bowl. Sift together tapioca, cornstarch, sugar, cinnamon and nutmeg in a separate bowl. Stir into pineapple mixture and blend in butter. Pour into pie crust and bake at 400 degrees for 10 minutes; reduce oven temperature to 375 degrees and bake an additional 20 minutes. Serves 8.

Tami Bowman
Gooseberry Patch

Maple-Pecan Pie
Peggy Bowman (Palisade, CO)

Great anytime, but just about perfect when served warm on a chilly autumn day.

4 eggs, beaten
⅔ c. sugar
½ t. salt
6 T. butter, softened

1 c. maple syrup
1½ c. pecan halves
9-inch pie crust
Garnish: whipped topping

Blend eggs, sugar, salt, butter and syrup in a bowl; set aside. Sprinkle pecan halves over pie crust; pour in syrup mixture. Bake at 375 degrees for 15 minutes; reduce oven temperature to 350 degrees and bake 25 more minutes, or until center is set. Cool on a wire rack. Serve with whipped topping. Serves 8.

Peanut Butter Strudel Pie

The best peanut butter pie! Topped with meringue, it's wonderful.

¼ c. peanut butter
¾ c. powdered sugar
9-inch pie crust, baked
½ c. all-purpose flour
⅔ c. plus ½ c. sugar, divided
¼ t. salt

2 c. milk, scalded
3 eggs, separated and divided
2 T. butter
½ t. vanilla extract
¼ t. cream of tartar
1 t. cornstarch

Mix peanut butter and powdered sugar together by hand in a small bowl until crumbly. Spread over bottom of pie crust, reserving about one tablespoon for topping. Mix flour, ⅔ cup sugar and salt in a saucepan; gradually add milk. Cook over medium heat until mixture thickens and boils, about 2 minutes. Remove from heat and set aside. Beat egg yolks and blend in a small amount of milk mixture; stir well. Return to pan and cook one minute. Add butter and vanilla; cool. Pour over peanut butter crumbs in pie crust. Beat egg whites until firm; add cream of tartar and beat until thick. Add remaining ½ cup sugar and cornstarch; beat until stiff. Spoon on top of pie. Be sure to seal the edges with the meringue to avoid spillover of pie contents. Bake at 425 degrees for 15 minutes, or until golden. Cool and serve. Serves 8.

Phyllis Laughrey
Mt. Vernon, OH

kitchen tip

To properly whip egg whites into a meringue, be sure to remove all of the yolk.

pie exchange

For a new twist, host a pie party and invite everyone to bring their best-loved pie to share. Bring home a brand-new recipe…it just might become a favorite!

Coconut-Caramel Crunch Pie

Toasted coconut and pecans give this tasty pie its delicious crunch.

¼ c. butter
½ c. chopped pecans
7-oz. pkg. flaked coconut
8-oz. pkg. cream cheese, softened
14-oz. can sweetened condensed milk
16-oz. container frozen whipped topping, thawed
2 9-inch deep-dish pie crusts, baked
caramel ice cream topping

Melt butter in a 10" skillet; add pecans and coconut. Cook, stirring frequently, until coconut is golden. Blend cream cheese and milk in a bowl; fold in whipped topping. Spread a quarter of the mixture into each pie crust; drizzle caramel topping on top. Sprinkle a quarter of the coconut and pecan mixture over each pie; repeat layers. Cover; freeze until firm. Let stand 5 minutes at room temperature before serving. Serves 16.

Valarie Dennard
Palatka, FL

Sweet Potato Pie

"An easy make-ahead pie...just bake a couple of days ahead and refrigerate. Not only will you save time, but I think it's tastier too."

—Barb

¼ c. butter, softened
⅓ c. honey
⅛ t. salt
2 c. sweet potatoes, cooked and mashed
3 eggs, beaten
½ c. milk
1 t. vanilla extract
½ t. cinnamon
½ t. nutmeg
½ t. ground ginger
8-inch pie crust
1 c. pecan halves

Blend butter, honey and salt in a large bowl; set aside. Combine sweet potatoes, eggs, milk, vanilla and spices in a separate bowl; stir into butter mixture. Pour into pie crust; sprinkle with pecan halves. Bake at 375 degrees for 50 to 55 minutes; cool. Store in refrigerator. Serves 8.

Barb Kietzer
Niles, MI

Coconut-Caramel
Crunch Pie

Brown Sugar Puddin' Pies

Brown Sugar Puddin' Pies

Bite-size, brown sugar pies…great for any get-together.

15-ct. pkg. mini phyllo shells, unbaked
½ c. butter, softened
¾ c. sugar
¾ c. brown sugar, packed
2 eggs
½ c. half-and-half
½ t. vanilla extract
Garnish: nutmeg and whipped topping

Place mini shells on an ungreased baking sheet. Bake at 350 degrees for 4 to 5 minutes; set aside. Blend butter and sugars in a bowl until light and fluffy; blend in eggs, half-and-half and vanilla. Spoon into pie crusts; sprinkle tops with nutmeg. Bake at 350 degrees for 15 to 20 minutes, until set. Top with a dollop of whipped topping and a dusting of nutmeg before serving. Serves 15.

Angela Nichols
Mt. Airy, NC

kitchen tip

Look for the mini phyllo shells in the freezer section of your local grocery store.

Crunchy Peanut Butter Pie

30 butter cookies, crushed
¼ c. butter, melted
2 T. water
¾ c. crunchy peanut butter
8-oz. pkg. cream cheese, softened
¼ c. butter, softened
1 c. powdered sugar
1 T. almond extract
1 c. frozen whipped topping, thawed
Optional: chopped nuts

Combine butter cookies, melted butter and water in a bowl; press into the bottom of a 9" deep-dish pie plate and set aside. Blend peanut butter and cream cheese in a bowl until smooth; add butter. Mix in powdered sugar and almond extract; blend well. Fold in whipped topping; spread into pie crust. If desired, sprinkle with chopped nuts; cover with plastic wrap and refrigerate at least 4 hours before serving. Serves 8.

Wendy Lee Paffenroth
Pine Island, NY

Crustless Pumpkin Pie

"My favorite pumpkin dessert...too good to save only for Thanksgiving!"

—Linda

4 eggs, beaten
15-oz. can pumpkin
12-oz. can evaporated milk
1½ c. sugar
2 t. pumpkin pie spice
1 t. salt

18½-oz. pkg. yellow cake mix
1 c. chopped pecans or
   walnuts
1 c. butter, melted
Optional: whipped topping,
   chopped nuts, cinnamon

Combine eggs, pumpkin, evaporated milk, sugar, spice and salt in a bowl. Mix well; pour into an ungreased 13"x9" baking pan. Sprinkle dry cake mix and nuts over top. Drizzle with butter; do not stir. Bake at 350 degrees for 45 minutes to one hour, or until a toothpick inserted in the center comes out clean. Serve with whipped topping; sprinkle with nuts and cinnamon. Serves 8 to 10.

Linda Webb
Delaware, OH

Butterscotch Pie

A creamy butterscotch custard...try topping it with whipped cream.

2 c. milk
3 egg yolks
¼ c. butter

1 T. all-purpose flour
1 c. brown sugar, packed
9-inch pie crust, baked

Whisk milk and egg yolks together in a bowl; pour into a saucepan. Cook over low heat until warmed; remove from heat. Brown butter in a deep skillet over medium-low heat; mix in flour until smooth. Blend in sugar until dissolved; slowly add milk mixture, stirring until thickened, about 5 minutes. Pour into pie crust; refrigerate until firm. Serves 8.

Dena Dukes
Secretary, MD

Glazed Apple-Cream Pie

In days gone by, a meal was never complete without the crowning touch of dessert. It was the moment to heap praise on the cook who was known for her special recipe…a recipe often not shared!

½ c. sugar
½ c. plus 2 T. milk, divided
½ c. whipping cream
¼ c. butter
2 T. cornstarch
1 t. vanilla extract

9-inch pie crust, baked
2 Granny Smith apples,
   peeled, cored and sliced
1 T. all-purpose flour
1 t. cinnamon
9-inch pie crust

tasty twist

Serve this pie à la mode.

Heat sugar, ½ cup milk, whipping cream and butter in a medium saucepan over low heat until butter is melted; while heating, combine remaining milk and cornstarch in a small bowl. Add to saucepan; heat until smooth, about 7 minutes. Remove from heat; add vanilla. Cool; pour into bottom of baked crust. Combine apples, flour and cinnamon in a separate bowl; sprinkle over filling. Top with remaining unbaked crust; flute edges. Vent top crust; cover edges with aluminum foil. Bake at 400 degrees for 45 to 50 minutes. Spread Topping on warm pie; refrigerate 1½ hours before serving. Serves 8.

Topping

½ c. powdered sugar
1 T. milk

¼ t. vanilla extract
1 T. butter, softened

Blend ingredients in a bowl until smooth.

Elizabeth Andrus
Gooseberry Patch

Luscious Blueberry Pie

"My grandmother was an expert baker, and this recipe is considered an heirloom in our family. You can purchase your pie crusts, but try Grandma's recipe when time allows."

—Deborah

2 pts. blueberries, washed and stems removed
1 c. sugar
2 T. all-purpose flour
⅛ t. cinnamon
1 T. lemon juice
⅛ t. salt
2 9-inch pie crusts
2 to 3 T. butter

Blend all ingredients except pie crusts and butter in a large bowl. Line a 9" pie plate with one crust; fill with blueberry filling and dot with butter. To prepare a lattice top, roll out remaining crust and cut into long strips ½-inch in width. On top of filled pie make an "X" with 2 strips in the center of the pie. Then, continue weaving strips, allowing space between each strip in a basket-weave pattern. When complete, trim any edges and crimp the lattice with the bottom crust. Bake at 425 degrees for 20 minutes; reduce the oven temperature to 350 degrees and bake an additional 40 minutes. Serves 8.

Pie Crust for Two-Crust Pie

2 c. all-purpose flour
1 t. salt
⅔ c. shortening
¼ c. cold water

Mix together flour and salt in a bowl; cut in shortening until mixture is the size of peas. Blend in water until flour is moistened and shape into a ball. Divide dough in half and roll out one portion at a time. If dough is too sticky, keep flouring hands, board and rolling pin. Makes 2 pie crusts.

Deborah Bassoff
Harrisburg, PA

flavor twist

Give fruit pies an extra burst of flavor! When making a favorite pie crust recipe, instead of using ice water, substitute the same amount of berry-flavored carbonated water.

Autumn Apple Pie

Cortland and Pippin apples are wonderful in this pie too.

½ c. plus 1 T. sugar, divided
6 Granny Smith apples,
　peeled, cored and thinly
　sliced
3 T. lemon juice
½ c. brown sugar, packed
2 t. cinnamon
¼ t. nutmeg
3 T. all-purpose flour
¼ c. butter, chilled and diced
9 caramels, unwrapped and
　quartered
2 9-inch pie crusts

Combine ½ cup sugar and all remaining ingredients except crusts in a large bowl. Stir until mixture evenly coats apples. Line a 9" pie plate with one pie crust; spoon filling into crust. Cover with second crust; flute edges and vent as desired. Sprinkle remaining sugar over crust. Place on an aluminum foil-lined baking sheet. Bake at 375 degrees for 30 minutes. Reduce oven temperature to 350 degrees; bake an additional 20 minutes, or until crust is golden. Serves 8.

Cheryl Musial
Acworth, GA

so thoughtful

Tell someone they're the apple of your eye! Paint a wooden box red, then paint on a cheerful greeting and stencil apples on the outside. Line with a bread cloth and fill with delicious apple crisp or cobbler—or this special apple pie!!

Raspberry-Cream Cheese Pie

Sweet berries with a chocolatey glaze...delicious!

tasty twist

Try a graham cracker crust instead of the chocolate cookie crust.

2 3-oz. pkgs. cream cheese, softened
14-oz. can sweetened condensed milk
1 egg
3 T. lemon juice
1 t. vanilla extract
1 c. raspberries
8-inch chocolate cookie crust
2 1-oz. sqs. semi-sweet baking chocolate
¼ c. whipping cream

Blend cream cheese in a bowl until light and fluffy; gradually add condensed milk. Mix in egg, lemon juice and vanilla; blend well. Arrange berries on bottom of pie crust; pour cream cheese mixture over berries. Bake at 350 degrees for 30 to 35 minutes, until set; cool completely. Melt chocolate with whipping cream in a double boiler over medium-low heat; stir until thick and smooth. Spread over top of pie; refrigerate until serving. Serves 8.

Rita Miller
Aberdeen, MD

Pear Pie

4 pears, peeled, cored and thinly sliced
3 T. frozen orange juice concentrate, thawed
9-inch pie crust
½ c. sugar
⅛ t. salt
¾ c. all-purpose flour
⅓ c. butter
2 t. cinnamon, divided

Toss pears and orange juice together; arrange in pie crust and set aside. Combine sugar, salt, flour, butter and one teaspoon cinnamon together until crumbly; layer over pears. Sprinkle with remaining cinnamon; bake at 400 degrees for about 40 minutes. Serves 8.

Fresh Peach Pie

There's nothing more delicious than warm, homemade peach pie topped with a big scoop of ice cream!

⅓ c. all-purpose flour
1 c. plus 1 T. sugar, divided
¼ c. butter
10 to 12 peaches, pitted,
   peeled and sliced

2 9-inch pie crusts
Optional: ice cream

Combine flour, one cup sugar and butter in a bowl until crumbly; set aside. Arrange a layer of peaches on bottom pie crust; sprinkle one tablespoon of flour mixture on top. Repeat layers until peaches and flour mixture are gone. Top with second crust; flute edges and vent. Sprinkle with remaining sugar; bake at 350 degrees for 45 minutes, or until crust is golden. Serve warm with a scoop of ice cream, if desired. Serves 8.

Gerri Phillips
Paoli, IN

Heartwarming Cherry Pie

"When this pie is done baking, sometimes I'll open the oven door and let it sit inside until it's just warm. Not only does it create extra warmth for the kitchen, but the aroma drifts through the entire house!"

—Susan

3 c. frozen pitted tart red
   cherries, thawed and juice
   reserved
1 c. sugar
½ t. salt
¼ c. all-purpose flour

1 T. butter
4 drops almond extract
4 drops vanilla extract
8 drops red food coloring
2 9-inch pie crusts

Pour cherry juice into a 2-quart saucepan; heat over medium heat. Whisk in sugar, salt and flour; heat until mixture thickens and becomes glossy. Remove from heat; mix in cherries, butter, extracts and food coloring. Pour into bottom pie crust. Add top crust; flute edges and vent top. Bake at 450 degrees for 10 minutes; reduce oven temperature to 350 degrees and continue baking for 40 to 45 minutes. Serves 8.

Susan Young
Madison, AL

Mom's Rhubarb Pie

1½ c. sugar
3 T. all-purpose flour
⅛ t. salt

2 eggs, beaten
3 c. rhubarb, chopped
2 9-inch pie crusts

Combine sugar, flour and salt in a bowl; mix well. Add eggs; blend until smooth. Fold in rhubarb. Place bottom pie crust in a 9-inch pie plate; pour into bottom pie crust. Top with second crust; flute edges and vent. Bake at 450 degrees for 10 minutes; reduce oven temperature to 350 degrees; cover pie edges with aluminum foil and bake an additional 30 minutes. Serves 8.

Crust

½ c. oil
¼ c. milk

2 c. all-purpose flour
⅛ t. salt

Mix oil and milk in a medium mixing bowl; set aside. Combine flour and salt in a small bowl; add to milk mixture. Divide dough in half; roll out each half on a lightly floured surface to a 9-inch circle. Makes two 9-inch crusts.

Mary Ann Nemecek
Springfield, IL

"Growing up, we always had rhubarb in the garden and my Grandpa Pop, who lived with us, took care of it. When Mom was a child, she remembered moving several times, but he always dug up the rhubarb patch and planted it once again at their new home!"

—Mary Ann

vary it up
There are lots of variations to the traditional rhubarb pie...try adding cherries, raisins or strawberries to the recipe for a whole new treat.

Blackberry Cobbler

A great recipe for all those fresh, juicy summer berries! Serve with scoops of vanilla ice cream and extra blackberries.

½ c. butter, melted
1 c. all-purpose flour
1 c. milk
1⅓ c. sugar, divided
2 t. baking powder

2 T. cornstarch
2 t. lemon juice
½ t. cinnamon
¼ t. nutmeg
2 c. blackberries

Spread melted butter in an 8"x8" baking pan. Blend flour, milk, one cup sugar and baking powder in a bowl; pour batter into pan. Combine remaining ⅓ cup sugar and remaining ingredients in a bowl and pour into center of batter; do not stir. Bake at 375 degrees for 45 minutes. Serves 6.

Diane Long
Delaware, OH

Raspberry Cobbler

1 c. all-purpose flour
¼ c. plus ½ T. sugar, divided
⅛ t. salt
½ c. unsalted butter, chilled
  and cut into pieces
1½ T. ice water
2 10-oz. pkgs. frozen whole
  unsweetened raspberries
2 T. whipping cream
Garnish: whipped cream

Combine flour, ½ tablespoon sugar and salt in a medium bowl. Cut in butter until mixture resembles coarse meal. Add water, a few drops at a time, just enough to hold dough together. Place the pastry on a lightly floured board and roll into a rectangle ⅛-inch thick; chill 20 minutes. Place raspberries in the bottom of a greased 11"x7" baking pan. Sprinkle evenly with half of remaining sugar. Place dough over raspberries; crimp edges. Cut steam vents in dough; brush with whipping cream and sprinkle with remaining sugar. Bake at 425 degrees for 25 minutes, or until pastry is golden brown and fruit juices are bubbling in the center. Serve warm with whipped cream. Serves 8.

Kathy McGuire
Wenonah, NJ

Buttery Blueberry Cobbler

Depending on what time of year it is, I've used fresh peaches or blackberries in this cobbler too.

½ c. butter, melted
1 c. all-purpose flour
1¼ c. sugar, divided
1 t. baking powder
½ c. milk
2 c. blueberries
1 T. lemon juice

Spread melted butter in an 8"x8" baking pan. Stir together flour, one cup sugar and baking powder in a bowl. Add milk and stir until batter is smooth. Pour evenly over butter in pan; do not stir. Mix berries, lemon juice and remaining sugar in a saucepan. Bring to a boil and pour evenly over butter and batter; do not stir. Bake at 350 degrees for 45 minutes. Serves 6.

Debra Thornton
DeMotte, IN

All-Star Cobbler

1¼ c. all-purpose flour
½ t. salt
½ c. shortening, chilled and
  cut into pieces
5 to 6 T. ice water
10-oz. pkg. frozen raspberries,
  thawed, juice reserved

¼ c. sugar
2 t. cornstarch
½ t. cinnamon
¼ t. nutmeg
2 apples, peeled, cored and
  sliced

Sift together flour and salt in a bowl; cut in shortening until mixture is crumbly. Add ice water, one tablespoon at a time, until dough comes together. Wrap dough in plastic wrap and chill one hour. Add reserved raspberry juice to a one-cup measuring cup; add enough water to equal one cup liquid. Combine sugar, cornstarch, cinnamon and nutmeg in a saucepan; blend in raspberry liquid. Bring to a boil over medium heat, stirring constantly, until mixture thickens. Remove from heat and stir in raspberries and apples. Pour cobbler filling into a greased 2-quart casserole dish; set aside. Remove dough from refrigerator and roll out to ¼-inch thickness; cut with a star-shaped cookie cutter. Place stars over raspberry and apple filling, overlapping if desired. Bake at 375 degrees for 25 to 30 minutes. Serves 6.

Coli Harrington
Delaware, OH

Mango Cobbler
Paula Chase (Aurora, CO)

2 c. mangoes, sliced
1¼ c. sugar, divided
1 c. all-purpose flour
1 T. baking powder
½ t. salt

4-oz. can evaporated milk
1 egg, beaten
½ c. butter, melted
cinnamon to taste

Place mangoes in a medium bowl; cover with water and sprinkle with ¼ cup sugar. Set aside. Combine remaining one cup sugar, flour, baking powder and salt in a bowl; add milk and egg and mix into a smooth batter. Spread melted butter in an 8"x8" baking pan. Pour batter over butter; add fruit (do not drain) and sprinkle with cinnamon. Bake at 350 degrees for 40 to 45 minutes. Top should be lightly golden and center should be firm. Serves 6.

Cookie Cobbler

So easy, even when you're short on time!

16-oz. can whole-berry
   cranberry sauce
⅓ c. brown sugar, packed
3 T. all-purpose flour
1 t. cinnamon

4 apples, peeled, cored, sliced
   and halved
½ of an 18-oz. pkg. refrigerated
   sugar cookie dough

    Blend together cranberry sauce, brown sugar, flour and cinnamon in
a mixing bowl; fold in apples and stir. Spread cobbler filling in the bottom
of a greased 13"x9" baking pan. Slice cookie dough into ¼-inch slices and
lay over filling. Bake at 400 degrees for 30 to 35 minutes, until apples are
tender. Serves 6.

Donna Dye
London, OH

Grandma's Easy Peach Cobbler

You can always count on this recipe; it's rich but oh-so good!

1 c. all-purpose flour
1 c. sugar
2 t. baking powder
½ c. milk

½ c. margarine, melted
29-oz. can sliced peaches,
 juice reserved

Combine flour, sugar and baking powder in a bowl; mix well. Blend milk into flour mixture until moistened. Pour into a greased 2-quart casserole dish or individual oven-proof skillets; add margarine. Pour peaches and reserved juice over batter; do not stir. Bake at 350 degrees for about 30 minutes. Serves 6.

Rene Ray
Delaware, OH

Cherry Cobbler

1 c. canned or frozen pitted
 cherries, drained, juice
 reserved
½ c. plus 1½ T. sugar, divided
1 c. plus 1 T. all-purpose flour,
 divided
¼ t. plus ⅛ t. salt, divided

¼ t. almond extract
red food coloring
1½ t. baking powder
3 T. margarine
⅓ c. milk
additional milk
sugar to taste

"One of my favorites because it seems just right after a meal; it's not too sweet, and it takes very little time to prepare."

—Karen

Spray an 8"x8" baking pan with non-stick vegetable spray. Place cherries in pan; set aside. Heat cherry juice, ½ cup sugar, one tablespoon flour and ⅛ teaspoon salt in a small saucepan over medium heat. Cook, stirring constantly, 2 minutes. Add almond extract and a few drops of food coloring; pour over cherries. Sift remaining flour with remaining salt, baking powder and remaining sugar in a bowl. Blend in margarine until crumbly; stir in milk. Drop by tablespoonfuls over cherry mixture; brush with milk and sprinkle with sugar to taste. Bake at 425 degrees for 15 to 20 minutes. Serves 6.

Karen Hess
Scott City, KS

Chestnut Farm Apple Crisp

Add a scoop of vanilla ice cream drizzled with warm caramel sauce!

½ c. butter, melted
1 c. brown sugar, packed
½ c. apple cider
½ c. all-purpose flour
1 t. cinnamon
½ t. baking powder
¼ t. salt

¼ t. mace
1 c. long-cooking oats
½ c. wheat germ
½ c. pecans, chopped
4 c. apples, peeled, cored and
   diced

Combine melted butter and brown sugar in a bowl; stir by hand until well blended. Stir in the cider, flour, cinnamon, baking powder, salt and mace; blend well. Add the oats, wheat germ and pecans; stir until blended. Gently fold in the apples. Spread in a greased 9"x9" baking pan. Bake at 350 degrees for 30 minutes, or until top is browned and looks crisp. Serves 8 to 12.

Beth Haney
Edwards, IL

Persimmon Crisp

6 c. ripe persimmons, sliced
1¼ t. cinnamon
¼ t. nutmeg
¾ c. milk
6 T. butter, softened and divided
2 eggs

1 c. sugar
1½ c. biscuit baking mix, divided
½ c. pecans, chopped
⅓ c. brown sugar, packed
Garnish: whipped cream or vanilla ice cream

"Beginning with a recipe that used apples, I made some changes and created this tasty persimmon crisp!"

—Rosalie

Mix persimmons and spices in a bowl and place in a greased 8"x8" baking pan. Blend milk, 2 tablespoons butter, eggs, sugar and ½ cup biscuit baking mix until smooth, about 15 seconds in a blender or one minute with an electric mixer. Pour over persimmons and spices. Mix together remaining biscuit baking mix, pecans, brown sugar and remaining butter in a bowl. Stir until crumbly and sprinkle over top. Bake at 325 degrees for one hour, or until a knife inserted in the center comes out clean. Cool and serve with whipped cream or vanilla ice cream. Serves 8.

Rosalie Benson
Martinez, CA

Crunchy Oat & Fruit Crisp

A crunchy, fruit-filled crisp that's tasty warm or cold.

1 c. quick-cooking oats
¾ c. brown sugar, packed and divided
5 T. all-purpose flour, divided
⅓ c. margarine, melted
1 c. blueberries

1 c. cherries
4 apples, peeled, cored and thickly sliced
¼ c. orange juice concentrate
1 T. cinnamon

Combine oats, ½ cup brown sugar, 2 tablespoons flour and margarine in a bowl; set aside. Combine fruit, juice, cinnamon, remaining ¼ cup brown sugar and remaining 3 tablespoons flour in a separate bowl. Stir until fruit is evenly coated. Spoon filling into a greased 8"x8" baking pan. Sprinkle topping over fruit mixture. Bake at 350 degrees for 30 to 35 minutes, until apples are tender and topping is golden brown. Serves 6.

Sandi Figura
Decatur, IL

Grandma Eddy's Apple Crumble

"An old family favorite that brings back memories of our visits to my husband's mother's and grandmother's homes."

—Mary

¾ c. margarine, softened
¾ c. all-purpose flour
¾ c. brown sugar, packed
¾ c. quick-cooking oats
⅛ t. salt

4 to 6 apples, peeled, cored and sliced
cinnamon to taste
¼ c. sugar

Mix margarine, flour, brown sugar, oats and salt in a bowl until crumbly; set aside. Place apples in a greased 13"x9" baking pan; sprinkle with cinnamon and sugar. Sprinkle topping over all and bake at 375 degrees for 30 minutes, or until topping is lightly browned and crunchy. Serves 6.

Mary Warren
Auburn, MI

Crunchy Oat
& Fruit Crisp

Apple Brown Betty

One of those time-tested recipes we all remember from childhood.

6 to 8 apples, peeled, cored
  and chopped
1 c. sugar
1 c. all-purpose flour
1 t. baking powder

1 t. salt
1 egg, beaten
2 T. butter, melted
cinnamon to taste

Place apples in a greased or parchment paper-lined 9"x9" baking pan; set aside. Mix sugar, flour, baking powder and salt in a bowl; stir in egg and place mixture on top of apples. Drizzle butter over top; sprinkle with cinnamon. Bake at 350 degrees for 45 minutes. Serves 6.

Terri Thompson
Middletown, CT

Pecan Tarts

"My mother is a fabulous cook and is known for her trademark goodies: these pecan tarts! When we had bake sales in high school, Mother always made these. They never actually made it to the table...the teachers were the first to buy them!"

—Frankie

3-oz. pkg. cream cheese,
  softened
½ c. margarine, softened
1 c. all-purpose flour
1 egg

¾ c. brown sugar, packed
½ t. salt
1 t. vanilla extract
¾ c. pecans, chopped

Combine cream cheese, margarine and flour in a bowl; chill one hour. Blend egg, brown sugar and salt in a separate bowl; mix well. Blend in vanilla and pecans. Roll dough into 24 balls. Press into tartlet pan and form into cups. Fill with pecan mixture. Bake at 325 degrees for 30 minutes. Cool slightly and remove from pans. Makes 2 dozen.

Frankie Stanley
Columbia, IL

Apple-Cranberry Crisp

6 c. Golden Delicious or
   Winesap apples, peeled,
   cored and sliced
3 c. cranberries
1 c. sugar
2 t. cinnamon

1 to 2 t. lemon juice
¾ c. butter, sliced and divided
1 c. all-purpose flour
1 c. brown sugar, packed
Garnish: vanilla ice cream

"A must-have at our
holiday dinners."

—*Brenda*

Toss together apple slices, cranberries, sugar and cinnamon in a large bowl. Spread in a greased 13"x9" baking pan. Sprinkle with lemon juice; dot with ¼ cup butter. Blend remaining butter with flour and brown sugar in a bowl until crumbly; sprinkle over apple mixture. Bake at 350 degrees for one hour. Serve warm with ice cream. Serves 10 to 12.

Brenda Derby
Northborough, MA

Chess Tarts

These tiny tarts are great for a holiday buffet table.

tasty twist

Top each tart with berries.

4 eggs
2 c. brown sugar, packed
2 T. all-purpose flour
6 T. unsalted butter, melted
1 T. vinegar

¼ c. whipping cream
1 t. lemon zest
10 refrigerated tart shells
10 nut halves

Beat eggs, brown sugar, flour, butter, vinegar, whipping cream and lemon zest in a bowl. Place tart shells on a baking sheet. Pour egg mixture into tart shells; top each with a nut half. Bake at 375 degrees for 10 minutes. Makes 10 tarts.

Liz Plotnick
Gooseberry Patch

Chocolate Tartlets

Delectable on a dessert buffet.

2 9-inch pie crusts
⅔ c. whipping cream
3 1-oz. sqs. semi-sweet baking
  chocolate, chopped

3 1-oz. sqs. sweet baking
  chocolate, chopped
Garnish: whipped cream,
  raspberries

Roll out pie crusts to ⅛-inch thick on a floured surface. Cut out 24 circles with a 2¾-inch round biscuit cutter. Fit carefully into mini muffin cups, pressing edges against rims and crimping with a fork. Bake at 350 degrees for 7 to 10 minutes, until set and golden. Cool. Bring whipping cream just to simmering in a saucepan over medium heat. Remove from heat; add chocolates and let stand 2 minutes. Whisk until melted; transfer to a medium bowl. Cover and chill one hour. Beat chocolate mixture with an electric mixer at medium speed until soft peaks form. Spoon into baked crusts; chill. At serving time, garnish with dollops of whipped cream and raspberries. Makes 2 dozen.

Emily Plotnick
West Linn, OR

Brown Sugar & Raisin Tarts

2 9-inch refrigerated pie
  crusts
1 c. raisins, finely chopped
½ c. walnuts, chopped
½ c. brown sugar, packed

3 T. butter, softened
3 T. orange juice
1 egg, beaten
2½ T. half-and-half
Garnish: whipped cream

"An old family recipe, handed down for many years...it's one of my husband's favorite recipes when he has a sweet tooth!"

—*Virginia*

Cut refrigerated pie crusts into 2-inch rounds using a small round biscuit cutter. Place in a mini muffin pan. Combine raisins, walnuts, brown sugar, butter, orange juice, egg and half-and-half in a bowl. Spoon mixture equally among tarts. Bake at 425 degrees for 20 minutes, or until pastry is lightly golden. Garnish with whipped cream. Makes one dozen small tarts.

Virginia Watson
Scranton, PA

Caramel-Nut Tart

To make each slice extra-special, top with a dollop of whipped cream and chocolate shavings.

make-ahead magic

Make this yummy tart the day before. Drizzle with chocolate right before serving.

3 c. pecans, chopped and divided
⅓ c. slivered almonds
3 T. sugar
⅓ c. butter, softened
1 t. vanilla extract

28 caramels, unwrapped
⅓ c. half-and-half
3 T. semi-sweet chocolate chips
1 t. oil

Process 1½ cups pecans, almonds and sugar in a food processor until finely ground, but not pasty; set aside. Blend together butter and vanilla in a bowl; add ground nut mixture. Gently press into the bottom of a greased 9" tart pan. Bake at 350 degrees for 20 minutes, or until golden. Remove to a wire rack and let cool completely. Combine caramels and half-and-half in a large saucapen and cook over medium heat until mixture is smooth. Spoon over crust; top with remaining pecans. Let caramel cool and set until firm, about 30 minutes. Melt together chocolate chips and oil in a small saucepan over medium heat; stir to blend and then drizzle over tart. Serves 12.

Lisa Watkins
Gooseberry Patch

Triple-Berry Tart

1 c. all-purpose flour
¼ c. plus 2 T. sugar, divided
¼ t. salt
½ c. butter, sliced
2 T. walnuts, finely chopped
1¾ c. plus 2 T. sour cream, divided
¼-oz. env. unflavored gelatin
5 T. water
½ c. blueberries
⅓ c. blackberries
⅓ c. raspberries
1 c. plain yogurt
½ t. vanilla extract
¼ c. plus 2 T. orange juice
2 T. brown sugar, packed
1 to 2 t. orange zest
Garnish: fresh berries and mint leaves

"Three of my favorite summertime berries are in this tart; our family thinks it's the best!"

—Gail

Combine flour, 2 tablespoons sugar and salt in a large bowl; cut in butter until crumbly. Stir in walnuts and 2 tablespoons sour cream, one tablespoon at a time, until dough forms a ball. Flatten ball slightly; wrap in plastic wrap. Refrigerate about 30 minutes. Roll out dough on a lightly floured surface into a 12-inch circle and place in a greased 9" tart pan with removable bottom. Bake at 350 degrees for 18 to 22 minutes, until lightly browned; set aside. Combine gelatin and water in a small saucepan. Cook over medium heat, stirring constantly, until gelatin is completely dissolved, about 2 to 3 minutes. Remove from heat. Combine blueberries, blackberries and raspberries in a blender. Cover; blend at high speed one minute or until puréed. Place in a medium bowl. Stir in remaining ¼ cup sugar, yogurt, ¾ cup sour cream and vanilla. Whisk in gelatin mixture and pour filling into crust. Cover and chill 3 hours. Stir together orange juice and brown sugar in a small bowl. Whisk in remaining one cup sour cream and orange zest. Cover and refrigerate 30 minutes. Spoon sauce over individual servings and garnish with fresh berries and mint leaves. Serves 8 to 10.

Gail Prather
Bethel, MN

Coffee-Nut Torte

6 eggs, separated
2 c. sugar
1 t. vanilla extract
1 c. coffee, cold and divided

1 c. walnuts, ground
2 c. all-purpose flour
1 T. baking powder

Blend egg yolks, sugar, vanilla and ¼ cup coffee in a large bowl; beat until thick. Combine walnuts, flour and baking powder in a separate bowl; add to egg mixture alternately with remaining coffee. Beat egg whites until stiff peaks form; fold into coffee mixture. Pour into 2 greased 9" round cake pans. Bake at 350 degrees for 25 minutes. Cool; spread with Frosting. Serves 16.

Frosting

½ c. brown sugar, packed
¼ c. milk
3 T. all-purpose flour
water

1 t. vanilla extract
½ t. maple flavoring
1 c. butter, softened
2 c. powdered sugar

Combine brown sugar, milk and flour in a saucepan; add enough water to form a paste. Stir in vanilla and maple flavoring; heat until thickened and then set aside to cool. Beat butter in a separate bowl; gradually mix in powdered sugar, blending well. Add cooled mixture; blend until light and fluffy.

Gail Foster
Leavittsburg, OH

kitchen tip

Does a pie recipe call for separating eggs? If so, they're easy to separate when cold, but for the best results, be sure to bring them back to room temperature before using them.

Rustic Pear Tart

Simple to prepare, this tart can make one large or many bite-size tarts!

1 c. plus 2 T. all-purpose flour, divided
¼ c. plus 1 T. plus 1 t. sugar, divided
¼ t. baking powder
¼ t. salt
¼ c. plus 1 t. unsalted butter, chilled, cut into pieces and divided
3 T. sour cream
1½ lbs. pears, peeled, cored and sliced
1 T. lemon juice
½ t. vanilla extract
2 t. powdered sugar

Sift together one cup flour, one teaspoon sugar, baking powder and salt in a bowl; cut in ¼ cup butter until mixture resembles coarse meal. Stir in sour cream with a fork until the mixture is very crumbly and fine. Cover dough and chill 30 minutes. Combine pears, lemon juice, ¼ cup sugar and vanilla in a bowl; toss to coat. Roll dough on a lightly floured surface to a 14-inch circle. Place circle on an ungreased baking sheet. Mix together remaining flour and remaining one tablespoon sugar, and sprinkle on the crust. Arrange the pear mixture over crust, leaving a 2-inch border all around. Moisten dough edges with water and fold dough in 2 inches over the pears. Dot the pears with remaining one teaspoon butter and bake at 400 degrees for 40 minutes, or until crust is golden. Cool 15 minutes and dust with powdered sugar. Serves 10 to 12.

Melody Taynor
Everett, WA

Crumbly Rhubarb Tart

1½ c. all-purpose flour,
  divided
1 t. baking powder
3 T. powdered sugar
⅔ c. butter, divided
1 egg, beaten

4 t. milk
3 c. rhubarb, diced
3-oz. pkg. strawberry gelatin
  mix
1 c. sugar

Sift together one cup flour, baking powder and powdered sugar in a bowl; cut in ⅓ cup butter. Stir in egg and milk to form a soft dough and pat into an oiled 11"x7" baking pan. Spoon rhubarb over crust; sprinkle dry gelatin over rhubarb. Combine remaining flour, remaining butter and sugar in a bowl until crumbly; sprinkle over rhubarb filling. Bake at 350 degrees for 45 to 50 minutes; cool completely. Serves 8 to 10.

Connie Bryant
Topeka, KS

"We love this treat warm from the oven! It's tart, so you can substitute raspberries if you'd prefer, but this is really good!"

—Connie

pie party

Set aside a sunny afternoon to host a pie party for friends and neighbors! Set several tables under shady trees and cover them with quilts or old-fashioned ticking. Ask friends to bring their favorite pie and the recipe to share, and you provide the coffee, milk, plates, cups and forks.

Glazed Strawberry Tart

Really show off this tart for special occasions…drizzle with melted chocolate or dust with powdered sugar!

kitchen tip

If the crust becomes warm, chill it 20 minutes before baking. It's key to keep the butter in the crust chilled.

1½ c. all-purpose flour
½ c. almonds, ground
⅓ c. sugar
½ t. salt
6 T. chilled butter, sliced
1 egg

1 t. almond extract
¾ c. strawberry jam
1 t. lemon juice
2 pts. strawberries, hulled and halved
Garnish: whipped topping

Stir together flour, almonds, sugar and salt in a large mixing bowl; cut butter into mixture until coarse crumbs form. Whisk together egg and almond extract in a separate bowl; stir into flour mixture until a dough forms. Shape into a flattened ball; wrap in plastic wrap and refrigerate overnight. Grease and flour a baking sheet; place dough in center. Pat into a 10-inch circle; form a ¾-inch high rim around the outside edge. Pierce bottom of dough with a fork; bake at 350 degrees for 25 minutes, or until golden. Cool 10 minutes on baking sheet on a wire rack; transfer crust to rack to cool completely. Melt jam with lemon juice in a small saucepan over low heat until spreadable; spread ½ cup jam mixture over crust. Arrange berry halves on top, cut-sides down; brush with remaining jam mixture. Serve with whipped topping. Serves 6 to 8.

Jo Ann
Gooseberry Patch

Rustic Peach Tart

Oh-so easy to make…you'll want to try other fruit too!

9-inch pie crust
¾ c. plus 2 T. sugar, divided
⅓ c. all-purpose flour
½ t. ground ginger
¼ t. nutmeg
16-oz. pkg. frozen sliced
  peaches

Roll out pie crust on a floured surface into a 12-inch circle. Place on an ungreased baking sheet and set aside. Mix ¾ cup sugar, flour and spices in a bowl; add frozen peach slices and toss to coat. Spoon peaches onto crust to within 2 inches of edge. Gently fold over edge of crust to form a 2-inch border, pleating as you go. Moisten crust edge with water; sprinkle with remaining sugar. Bake at 425 degrees until golden, about 15 minutes; reduce oven temperature to 350 degrees. Bake until bubbly, about 30 to 35 minutes. Serves 8.

Jeni Steenblock
Des Moines, IA

Cherry-Chip
Bread, page 158

homemade breads + coffee cakes

Nothing is more inviting than the smell of freshly baked bread or coffee cake. Warm your soul with recipes like Raspberry Coffee Cake, Cinnamon Twist Bread, Farmhouse Buttermilk Bread and more!

Sour Cream-Cinnamon Coffee Cake

"Whenever we have guests, I serve this moist coffee cake for breakfast. It's a recipe I know I can always count on."

—Karen

1¾ c. sugar, divided
1 c. butter, softened
2 eggs
½ pt. sour cream
2 c. all-purpose flour
1½ t. baking powder
½ t. baking soda
1 t. vanilla extract
1 c. nuts, chopped
2 t. cinnamon

Combine 1¼ cups sugar, butter and eggs in a large bowl. Beat with an electric mixer at medium speed until fluffy; blend in sour cream. Sift together flour, baking powder and baking soda in a separate bowl; add to butter mixture. Add vanilla and blend well. Spoon half the mixture into a greased and floured 10" tube pan. Mix nuts, cinnamon and remaining sugar in a small bowl. Sprinkle half the nut mixture over batter. Repeat layers. Bake at 350 degrees for one hour. Serves 10.

Karen Moran
Navasota, TX

Sugar-Topped Coffee Cake

2 c. all-purpose flour
1 t. baking powder
½ t. baking soda
½ t. salt
1¼ c. sugar, divided
5 T. butter, softened
2 eggs
1 t. vanilla extract
1 c. sour cream
¾ c. walnuts, coarsely chopped
⅓ c. mini chocolate chips
1½ T. baking cocoa
¾ t. cinnamon
Garnish: powdered sugar

Blend together flour, baking powder, baking soda and salt in a large bowl. In a separate bowl, mix together one cup sugar and butter. Beat in eggs, one at a time; stir in vanilla. Add alternately with sour cream to dry ingredients; set aside. Mix walnuts, chocolate chips, remaining sugar, cocoa and cinnamon. Spoon half the batter into a greased and floured tube or Bundt® pan. Sprinkle half the nut mixture evenly over batter. Top with remaining batter; sprinkle remaining walnut mixture on top. Swirl batter with a butter knife to make a marbled coffee cake. Bake at 350 degrees for about 40 to 50 minutes. Cool completely and dust with powdered sugar. Serves 12.

Tina Wright
Atlanta, GA

Spicy Buttermilk Coffee Cake

Fills the house with a wonderful aroma while it's baking…it's sure to please everyone!

kitchen tip

Use a vintage cake stand instead of a plate to present this yummy treat.

2½ c. all-purpose flour
2 t. cinnamon, divided
½ t. salt
¼ t. ground ginger
1 c. brown sugar, packed
¾ c. sugar

¾ c. oil
1 c. walnuts, chopped
1 t. baking soda
1 t. baking powder
1 egg, beaten
1 c. buttermilk

Mix flour, one teaspoon cinnamon, salt, ginger, brown sugar, sugar and oil in a bowl. Remove ¾ cup of this mixture to a separate bowl; add walnuts and remaining one teaspoon cinnamon. Mix well and set aside. To the remaining batter, add baking soda, baking powder, egg and buttermilk; mix. Pour batter into a well-greased 13"x9" baking pan; sprinkle walnut mixture evenly over top. Bake at 350 degrees for 35 to 40 minutes. Serves 12.

Sue Collins
Valencia, CA

Coffee Cake Crescents

1 env. active dry yeast
2 T. warm water (110 to
   115 degrees)
1 c. less 2 T. milk
4 c. all-purpose flour
1 c. butter or margarine

1 c. plus 1 T. sugar, divided
1 t. salt
3 eggs, separated
1 T. cinnamon
Optional: ½ c. finely chopped
   walnuts

"Handed-down recipes
are always special...
this is my mother's."

—Liz

Sprinkle yeast over warm water in a glass measuring cup and add enough milk to make one cup; set aside. Combine flour, butter, one tablespoon sugar and salt in a large mixing bowl; set aside. Beat 3 egg yolks in a small bowl; stir into yeast mixture. Add yeast mixture to flour mixture; blend well. Cover dough and chill in refrigerator overnight. Separate dough into thirds; roll out each third into a ¼-inch thick rectangle; set aside. Beat 3 egg whites and remaining sugar in a bowl; spread evenly over each rectangle. Sprinkle with cinnamon and chopped nuts, if desired. Shape into crescent shapes; place on ungreased baking sheets and let rise one hour (dough will not double in bulk). Bake at 325 degrees for 30 minutes, or until golden brown. While baking, prepare Frosting; drizzle with Frosting while cake is still warm. Makes 3 large crescents.

Frosting

1 c. powdered sugar
1 T. butter, softened

2 T. milk

Combine all ingredients in a small bowl and blend well, adjusting milk and powdered sugar to desired consistency.

Liz Marcellin
Newark, CA

Apple-Oatmeal Coffee Cake

A tasty coffee cake any time of year, but especially good with just-picked apples from the orchard.

kitchen tip

Granny Smith, Gala or Honeycrisp apples are the best varieties for this recipe.

1 c. all-purpose flour
¾ t. baking soda
½ t. salt
¼ t. allspice
¼ t. cinnamon
1 c. sugar
1 c. quick-cooking oats

½ c. oil
1 egg
1 t. vanilla extract
1 c. apple, peeled, cored and chopped
⅓ c. nuts, chopped

Mix dry ingredients together in a large bowl. Add remaining ingredients; mixture will be quite thick. Pour into a greased 8"x8" baking pan. Bake at 350 degrees for 35 minutes. Serves 9.

Winnette Anker
South Holland, IL

Cherry Coffee Cake

The term "coffee cake" refers to a cake best enjoyed alongside a cup of coffee. They rarely contain actual coffee.

2 env. active dry yeast
⅔ c. warm water (110 to 115 degrees)
18¼-oz. box yellow cake mix, divided
2 eggs
1 c. all-purpose flour

14½-oz. can cherry pie filling
2 T. sugar
5 T. margarine, melted
1 c. powdered sugar
1 T. water
1 T. corn syrup

kitchen tip

The yeast gives this coffee cake a light texture, and we think the cherry pie filling makes it extra special!

Blend yeast into warm water in a large bowl until yeast is dissolved. Add 1½ cups cake mix, eggs and flour to yeast mixture. Beat with an electric mixer at medium speed 2 minutes. Spread batter in a greased 13"x9" baking pan. Top with pie filling and sprinkle with sugar. Mix remaining cake mix and margarine in a bowl until crumbly; sprinkle over pie filling. Bake at 375 degrees for 30 minutes. Mix together powdered sugar, water and corn syrup in a small bowl; drizzle over warm cake. Serves 12.

Gloria Kaufmann
Orrville, OH

Raspberry Coffee Cake

Your home will smell wonderful while this is baking.

2¼ c. all-purpose flour
1 c. sugar, divided
¾ c. margarine
¾ t. baking powder
½ t. baking soda
¼ t. salt
¾ c. sour cream

1 t. almond extract
2 eggs, divided
8-oz. pkg. cream cheese,
  softened
½ c. raspberry preserves
½ c. sliced almonds
Garnish: raspberries

Grease and flour bottom and sides of a 9" or 10" springform pan. Combine flour and ¾ cup sugar in a large bowl. Cut in margarine with a pastry blender or fork until mixture resembles coarse crumbs. Reserve one cup crumb mixture in a small bowl. Add baking powder, baking soda, salt, sour cream, almond extract and one egg to remaining crumb mixture; blend well. Spread batter over bottom and 2 inches up sides of pan. Batter should be about ¼ inch thick on sides. Combine cream cheese, remaining sugar and remaining egg in a small bowl; blend well. Pour into batter-lined pan. Carefully spoon preserves evenly over cream cheese mixture. Add sliced almonds to reserved crumb mixture. Sprinkle over preserves. Bake at 350 degrees for 45 to 55 minutes, until cream cheese filling is set and crust is deep golden brown. Cool 15 minutes. Remove sides of pan. Garnish with raspberries. Serves 16.

Susan Brzozowski
Ellicott City, MD

have a laugh

Do you have an album full of old photos from school? Pull out all the funniest ones…slumber parties, proms or band camp. Make color copies and slip them into invitations for all your girlfriends. Enjoy coffee and dessert together…and a lot of laughs too.

Fruit Coffee Cake

"My aunt Jean gave me this recipe when I was about 13 years old. I like it because it's easy to make and most of the ingredients are always in my kitchen pantry."

—Georgia

1 c. butter, softened
1 c. sugar
3 eggs
2 T. milk
1 t. vanilla extract

2 c. all-purpose flour
2 t. baking soda
⅛ t. salt
21-oz. can fruit pie filling
Garnish: powdered sugar

Combine butter and sugar in a large bowl. Blend in eggs, milk and vanilla. Sift together flour, baking soda and salt in a separate bowl. Add to egg mixture; blend well. Spread three-fourths of batter in a greased and floured 13"x9" baking pan. Spread fruit filling over batter; top with remaining batter. Sprinkle entire top with powdered sugar and bake at 350 degrees for 45 minutes. Serves 10.

Georgia Zerbe
South Bend, IN

Blueberry Cream Coffee Cake

⅔ c. plus 2 T. sugar, divided
¼ c. butter, softened
1 egg
¼ t. lemon extract
1 c. plus 3 T. all-purpose flour, divided
½ T. baking powder

½ t. salt
½ t. cinnamon, divided
½ c. milk
1 c. blueberries
4 oz. cream cheese, cubed
1 T. chilled butter

"A traditional recipe, but still a favorite of mine!"

—Stephanie

Beat ⅔ cup sugar and butter in a large bowl until light and fluffy. Blend in egg and lemon extract. Combine one cup flour, baking powder, salt and ¼ teaspoon cinnamon in a separate bowl. Add flour mixture alternately with milk to butter mixture. Toss blueberries with one tablespoon flour. Fold blueberries and cream cheese into batter; pour into a greased and floured 9" round cake pan. Combine remaining sugar, remaining flour and remaining cinnamon in a small bowl. Cut in butter until mixture resembles coarse crumbs. Sprinkle evenly over batter. Bake at 375 degrees for 30 minutes, or until a toothpick inserted in the center comes out clean. Serves 6.

Stephanie Moon
Boise, ID

double up

Double the ingredients and make a second coffee cake to give to your neighbor.

Applechip Coffee Cake

Use different types of apple to change the taste…spicy Fuji, crunchy Red Delicious or tart Granny Smith.

1½ c. plus 2 T. all-purpose
  flour, divided
¾ c. sugar, divided
2 t. baking powder
1 t. salt
1 egg, beaten

½ c. milk
¼ c. oil
1 c. apple, peeled, cored and
  finely chopped
2 t. cinnamon
2 T. butter

Mix 1½ cups flour, ½ cup sugar, baking powder and salt in a large bowl. Blend together egg, milk, oil and apple in a separate bowl. Slowly add to dry ingredients. Spread batter into a greased 9"x9" baking pan. Blend together remaining flour, remaining sugar, cinnamon and butter in a small bowl. Sprinkle topping over cake. Bake at 400 degrees for 25 to 30 minutes. Serves 8.

Glenda Hill
Columbus, OH

Cherry-Chip Bread

Great flavors…almost like a chocolate-covered cherry!

2 c. all-purpose flour
1 c. sugar
1½ t. baking powder
½ t. baking soda
½ t. salt
¼ c. margarine

¾ c. water
1 egg, beaten
¾ c. maraschino cherries,
  drained and chopped
½ c. mini chocolate chips

Combine flour, sugar, baking powder, baking soda and salt in a large bowl. Cut in margarine until mixture resembles coarse meal. Stir in water and egg; fold in cherries and chips. Pour batter into a lightly oiled 9"x5" loaf pan. Bake at 350 degrees for 50 to 60 minutes. Cool in pan 10 minutes; remove from pan and cool completely on a wire rack. Serves 8.

Vicki Grounds
Woodland Park, CO

Cherry-Chip Bread

Orange-Nut Bread

"We like to serve this for a leisurely breakfast or brunch."

—The Governor's Inn

2 c. all-purpose flour
1 t. baking powder
½ t. salt
¼ t. baking soda
⅔ c. sugar
⅓ c. unsalted butter, softened

2 eggs
½ c. orange juice with pulp
½ c. water
½ t. vanilla extract
½ t. orange extract
1 c. walnuts, chopped

Grease three 6"x3½" loaf pans; set aside. Sift together flour, baking powder, salt and baking soda in a medium bowl. Blend sugar and butter in a large bowl. Beat in eggs, one at a time. Stir in orange juice and water alternately with flour mixture. Add extracts and walnuts; pour into pans. Bake at 350 degrees for 40 to 45 minutes. Remove from pans, cool and wrap. Chill well before serving. Serve with Orange-Cream Cheese Spread. Makes 3 small loaves.

Orange-Cream Cheese Spread

3 8-oz. pkgs. cream cheese, softened
3 to 4 T. powdered sugar

1 navel orange, unpeeled and chopped

Combine all ingredients in a food processor with steel blade in place. Process to a thick spread. Refrigerate several hours to blend flavors.

The Governor's Inn
Ludlow, VT

put it up

Pressed-glass jars can store everything from flour and sugar to cookie cutters and tins of sprinkles! Easily found at tag sales or flea markets, they'll bring back fond memories of Mom's kitchen!

Cinnamon Twist Bread

This is for those mornings when cold cereal just won't work!

2 c. all-purpose flour
1 c. plus 2 T. sugar, divided
4 t. baking powder
2½ t. cinnamon, divided
1¼ t. salt

1 c. buttermilk
⅓ c. oil
2 t. vanilla extract
2 eggs
2 t. butter, softened

Grease and flour bottom only of a 9"x5" loaf pan. Combine flour, one cup sugar, baking powder, 1½ teaspoons cinnamon, salt, buttermilk, oil, vanilla and eggs in a large bowl. Beat with an electric mixer at medium speed 3 minutes; pour batter into pan. Combine butter, remaining sugar and remaining cinnamon in a small bowl. Sprinkle over batter and swirl lightly to marble. Bake at 350 degrees for 45 to 50 minutes, until a toothpick inserted in the center comes out clean. Remove from pan before slicing. Serves 8.

Emily Nelsen
Jerome, ID

Walnut and Pumpkin Bread

2 c. all-purpose flour
2 t. baking powder
1 t. cinnamon
½ t. baking soda
½ t. salt
½ t. allspice
½ t. nutmeg

1 c. sugar
1 c. pumpkin
½ c. milk
2 eggs, beaten
½ c. butter, softened
1 c. walnuts, chopped

Sift together all dry ingredients in a large bowl; add pumpkin and milk. Beat in eggs, one at a time. Stir in butter and walnuts. Pour into 2 well-greased 9"x5" loaf pans. Bake at 350 degrees for 45 to 50 minutes, until a toothpick inserted in the center comes out clean. Serves 12.

Christine Sullivan
San Ramon, CA

Banana + Walnut Bread

make-ahead magic

A fruit-filled quick bread!
It's easily doubled and frozen.

¼ c. shortening
¼ c. margarine
1 c. sugar
2 eggs
1 c. bananas, mashed
1½ c. all-purpose flour
1 t. baking soda

¼ t. salt
¼ t. cinnamon
½ c. quick-cooking oats,
   uncooked
½ c. blueberries
½ c. walnuts, chopped

Combine shortening, margarine and sugar in a large bowl. Add eggs, one at a time, mixing well after each addition; stir in bananas. Sift together flour, baking soda, salt and cinnamon in a separate bowl. Stir oats, blueberries and nuts into dry ingredients. Carefully blend the dry mixture into the shortening mixture, stirring only to moisten. Pour batter into a well-greased 9"x5" loaf pan. Bake at 350 degrees for 50 to 55 minutes, until a toothpick inserted in the center comes out clean. Cool 10 minutes before removing from pan. Allow bread to cool completely on a wire rack. Serves 8.

Corky Hines
Walworth, NY

Strawberry Bread

3 c. all-purpose flour
2 c. sugar
1 t. baking soda
1 t. salt
1 t. cinnamon

4 eggs, beaten
1¼ c. oil
2 10-oz. pkgs. frozen
   strawberries, thawed and
   chopped

Combine flour, sugar, baking soda, salt and cinnamon in a large bowl; make a well in the center. Set aside. Mix remaining ingredients together in a separate bowl; pour into flour well. Stir until combined; divide batter and spread into 2 greased and floured 9"x5" loaf pans. Bake at 350 degrees for one hour; cool in pans 10 minutes. Remove from pans and cool on wire racks. Serves 16.

Terry Kokko
Parris Island, SC

Peanut Butter Bread
Michele Cutler (Sandy, UT)

A yummy bread we love to enjoy fresh out of the oven on cold, wintry days.

¾ c. sugar
½ c. peanut butter
1 t. vanilla extract
1¾ c. milk

2¼ c. all-purpose flour
4 t. baking powder
½ t. salt

Blend together sugar, peanut butter and vanilla in a large bowl. Gradually pour in milk; mix well. Sift together flour, baking powder and salt in a separate bowl; add to peanut butter mixture. Spread batter into a greased 9"x5" loaf pan. Bake at 350 degrees for 45 to 50 minutes. Serves 8.

Chocolate-Zucchini Bread

For variety, substitute one tablespoon orange extract for vanilla.

3 eggs
1 c. oil
2 c. sugar
2 t. vanilla extract
2½ c. all-purpose flour
2½ t. baking powder
1½ t. baking soda
1 t. salt
½ c. baking cocoa
2 c. zucchini, shredded
1 c. chopped nuts

Blend together eggs, oil and sugar in a large mixing bowl; add vanilla, flour, baking powder, baking soda, salt and cocoa, mixing well. Fold in zucchini and nuts; spoon into 2 greased 9"x5" loaf pans. Bake at 350 degrees for one hour. Makes 2 loaves; serves 16.

Janet Shelly
Bourbonnais, IL

Vermont Graham Bread

"A great old-fashioned bread my grandmother always made."

—Denise

3 c. milk, scalded
½ c. unsalted butter
1 T. salt
½ c. molasses
2 env. active dry yeast
⅓ c. warm water (110 to 115 degrees)
5 c. graham flour
4 c. all-purpose flour

Pour milk into a large bowl and cool slightly; stir in butter, salt and molasses. When mixture has cooled to warm, sprinkle yeast over warm water in a small bowl; stir to dissolve. Pour yeast mixture into milk mixture; add graham flour until well combined. Cover and let rise 45 minutes to one hour. Punch dough down and add all-purpose flour; dough will be soft. Let rise again until double in bulk. Divide dough in half and place each half in an oiled 9"x5" loaf pan. Cover and let rise until double in bulk. Bake at 375 degrees for 35 to 40 minutes. Makes 2 loaves; serves 16.

Denise Jones
Barre, VT

Glazed Lemon Bread

Very moist…enjoy it warm from the oven.

¾ c. shortening
1½ c. sugar
3 eggs
2¼ c. all-purpose flour

¼ t. baking soda
¼ t. salt
¾ c. buttermilk
zest of one lemon

Blend together shortening and sugar in a large bowl; add eggs, one at a time, beating well after each addition. Combine flour, baking soda and salt in a separate bowl; add to sugar mixture. Stir in buttermilk and zest. Divide between 2 greased 9"x5" loaf pans; bake at 350 degrees for 30 to 35 minutes. Pour Glaze over the tops of loaves while still warm. Makes 2 loaves; serves 16.

Glaze

¾ c. sugar   juice of one lemon

Stir together sugar and lemon juice in a small bowl until smooth.

Denise Pawlak
Grinnell, IA

tasty twist

Add lime zest to make it lemon-lime bread.

Coffee-Can Molasses Bread

Megan Brooks (Antioch, TN)

2 c. whole-wheat flour
½ c. cornmeal
2 t. baking soda
½ t. salt

2 c. buttermilk
½ c. molasses
½ c. raisins
½ c. dried apples, finely chopped

Combine all ingredients in a large bowl. Grease and flour 2 one-pound coffee cans; divide batter equally and spoon inside; let stand 30 minutes. Bake at 350 degrees for 50 to 55 minutes, until the top is golden and a knife inserted in the center comes out clean. Remove cans from oven and let cool 15 minutes. Remove loaves from cans and cool completely. Makes 2 loaves; serves 16.

Pennsylvania Dutch Loaves

Give a tasty gift! Just wrap these old-fashioned loaves in a square of homespun, then tuck them in a yellowware bowl.

4½ to 5 c. all-purpose flour, divided
1 env. active dry yeast
1¼ c. milk
½ c. butter
¾ c. sugar
1 t. salt
1 egg, beaten
¾ c. raisins
½ c. currants
⅓ c. candied citron, finely chopped
1 c. powdered sugar
¼ t. vanilla extract
1 to 2 T. milk
Garnish: ½ c. blanched almonds, finely chopped

Combine 2 cups flour and yeast in a large bowl. Heat milk, butter, sugar and salt in a saucepan over medium heat just until warm and butter is almost melted. Stir butter mixture into flour mixture; add egg. Beat with an electric mixer at low speed one minute, scraping sides of bowl. Beat at high speed 3 minutes. Add raisins, currants and citron; mix well. Stir in enough remaining flour by hand to make a moderately soft dough. Turn out onto a lightly floured surface; knead 5 to 8 minutes, until smooth and elastic. Place dough in a lightly greased bowl; turn once to grease surface. Cover and let rise about one hour. Divide dough among 4 mini loaf pans. Bake at 375 degrees for 20 to 30 minutes, until loaves sound hollow when lightly tapped. Set aside to cool. Sift powdered sugar in a medium bowl; add vanilla and enough milk until mixture reaches a drizzling consistency. Spoon over loaves and sprinkle with almonds. Makes 4 loaves; serves 16.

Tina Knotts
Gooseberry Patch

Old-Fashioned Honey Bread

A hearty bread that's easy to make. Great sliced for sandwiches or with a bowl of homemade soup.

make-ahead magic

Make this hearty loaf on Sunday and enjoy it throughout the week.

1½ c. water
8 oz. small-curd cottage cheese
½ c. honey
¼ c. plus 2 T. butter, divided
1 c. whole-wheat flour

2 T. sugar
2 env. active dry yeast
5½ to 6 c. all-purpose flour
1 T. salt
1 egg

Heat water, cottage cheese, honey and ¼ cup butter in a medium saucepan over medium heat until very warm. Combine warm liquid, whole-wheat flour, sugar, yeast, 2 cups all-purpose flour, salt and egg in a large bowl; beat with an electric mixer at medium speed 2 minutes. Stir in enough remaining flour by hand to make a stiff dough. Knead dough on a well-floured surface until smooth and elastic, about 2 minutes. Place in a greased bowl, turning to coat. Cover and let rise in a warm place until double in bulk, 45 to 60 minutes. Punch down dough; divide and shape into 2 loaves. Place in 2 greased 9"x5" loaf pans. Cover and let rise again until light and double in bulk, 45 to 60 minutes. Bake at 350 degrees for 40 to 50 minutes, until deep golden brown and loaves sound hollow when tapped. Immediately remove from pans. Brush warm loaves with remaining butter. Makes 2 loaves; serves 16.

Rene Ray
Delaware, OH

come here, honey

Make some honey butter: ¼ cup honey, 1 cup butter and ¼ cup powdered sugar. Blend and spoon into an old-fashioned crock or canning jar. A sweet way to say "thank you" to a friend.

English Muffin Loaf

6 c. all-purpose flour, divided
2 env. instant yeast
1 T. sugar
2 t. salt
¼ t. baking soda
2 c. milk
½ c. water
2 T. cornmeal, divided

Sift together 3 cups of flour with other dry ingredients in a large bowl. Heat milk and water to 120 to 130 degrees in a saucepan over medium heat. Add to dry mixture; beat well. Stir in remaining flour to make a stiff batter. Sprinkle one tablespoon cornmeal in the bottom of each of 2 greased 8½"x4½" loaf pans; spoon in batter over cornmeal. Cover and let rise in a warm place 45 minutes. Bake at 400 degrees for 25 minutes. Remove loaves from pans and cool on wire racks. Makes 2 loaves; serves 16.

Valerie Busch
Cygnet, OH

Anadama Bread

A hearty brown bread with a crunchy crust and soft inside.

½ c. cornmeal
2 c. boiling water
2 T. shortening
½ c. molasses
1 t. salt

1 pkg. cake yeast
½ c. warm water (110 to
    115 degrees)
6 c. all-purpose flour

   Stir cornmeal slowly into boiling water in a large heat-proof bowl; mix well. Add shortening, molasses and salt; set aside to cool. Dissolve yeast in warm water, about 5 minutes. Add yeast mixture alternately with flour to lukewarm cornmeal mixture. Knead until smooth and place in a large greased bowl. Set in a warm place; cover and let rise until double in bulk. Turn out onto a floured surface; divide in half. Knead and shape into 2 loaves. Place in 2 greased 9"x5" loaf pans and let rise again until double in bulk. Bake at 375 degrees for one hour. Makes 2 loaves; serves 16.

April Hale
Kirkwood, NY

Farmhouse Buttermilk Bread

The best bread for a sandwich…soft and so tasty!

kitchen tip

Give the yeast enough time to bloom. Once it's frothy and bubbly, it's ready to make bread.

2 env. active dry yeast
1 t. sugar
1 c. warm water (110 to 115 degrees)
1½ c. buttermilk
3 T. molasses
3 T. oil
1 T. salt
½ c. bran
2 c. whole-wheat flour
4 to 4½ c. bread flour

Dissolve yeast and sugar in warm water in bowl of a heavy-duty mixer; set aside 5 to 10 minutes. Blend in buttermilk, molasses, oil and salt. Gradually beat bran and whole-wheat flour into yeast mixture. Stir in bread flour, ½ cup at a time, until a stiff dough forms. Knead dough until smooth, adding more bread flour if dough is sticky. Place dough in an oiled bowl, turning once to coat all sides. Cover and let rise until double in bulk, about one hour. Punch down and knead lightly. Divide dough in half and place each half in an oiled 9"x5" loaf pan. Let rise until almost double in bulk, about one hour. Bake at 400 degrees for 45 to 50 minutes. Makes 2 loaves; serves 16.

Cindy Watson
Gooseberry Patch

spirit of giving

Wrap a loaf of bread in a quick and easy bread cloth. Begin with a 20-inch square of unbleached muslin, then use a permanent pen to write a message or favorite quote around the edges.

Sweet Corn-Buttermilk Bread

You can bake this in old-fashioned corn muffin pans or in a cast-iron skillet; just cut into wedges and serve.

1¼ c. cornmeal
1 c. all-purpose flour
⅔ c. sugar
⅔ c. brown sugar, packed
1 t. baking soda

½ t. salt
1 egg
1 c. buttermilk
¾ c. oil

Stir together cornmeal, flour, sugar, brown sugar, baking soda and salt in a bowl. Whisk together egg, buttermilk and oil in a separate bowl. Add to dry ingredients all at once, stirring just until blended. Spoon into a well-greased 9" round cake pan. Bake at 425 degrees for 20 minutes, or until golden brown. Serves 10.

Christy Doyle
Baton Rouge, LA

Irish Soda Bread

Since my sister Joan gave me this recipe, it's become my favorite!

4 c. all-purpose flour
¼ c. sugar
1 t. baking powder
2 T. caraway seeds
¼ c. butter

2 c. raisins
1⅓ c. buttermilk
1 egg
1 t. baking soda
1 egg yolk, beaten

Mix flour, sugar and baking powder in a large bowl; stir in caraway seeds. Cut in butter until mixture resembles coarse meal. Stir in raisins and set aside. Combine buttermilk, egg and baking soda in a small bowl; stir into flour mixture just until dry ingredients are moistened. Turn out onto a floured surface and knead lightly until dough is smooth. Shape into a ball and place in a greased 2-quart casserole dish. Brush with egg yolk and bake at 375 degrees for one hour. Cool bread 10 minutes before removing from casserole dish. Serves 8.

Claire McGeough
Lebanon, NJ

Country Cheddar Loaf

Country Cheddar Loaf

4 c. all-purpose flour, divided

2 T. sugar

1 env. instant yeast

1 t. salt

1 c. plus 1 T. water, divided

⅓ c. milk

2 c. Cheddar cheese, grated

1 egg white

Combine 1½ cups flour, sugar, yeast and salt in a large bowl. Heat one cup water and milk in a small saucepan over medium heat to 120 to 130 degrees; stir into dry ingredients. Stir in enough remaining flour to make a soft dough. Knead on a lightly floured surface until smooth and elastic. Cover; let rest on floured surface 10 minutes. Knead in cheese. Divide dough into 3 equal pieces; roll each piece into a 14-inch rope. Braid ropes, pinch ends to seal and place on a greased baking sheet. Cover and let rise 30 to 45 minutes. Beat egg white with remaining water in a small bowl; brush loaf with egg mixture. Bake at 375 degrees for 30 to 35 minutes. Remove from oven and allow to cool. Serves 12.

Holly Welsch
Delaware, OH

"It gives me such satisfaction to make my own bread, and this is a family favorite; we all have difficulty waiting for the bread to cool before we slice it! Our family enjoys it with a hot bowl of chicken noodle soup or a hearty bowl of chili."

—Holly

Onion & Sour Cream Bread

Let the bread machine do the hard work, then finish baking the bread in the oven. Nothing beats the taste of homemade whole-wheat bread!

3 c. whole-wheat flour

2 T. sugar

2 t. active dry yeast

1 t. salt

1-oz. pkg. dried onion soup mix

1 c. sour cream

½ c. water

Using your manufacturer's manual as a guide, place flour, sugar, yeast, salt, dried soup mix, sour cream and water in your bread machine. Select the manual or dough cycle and let the machine mix and knead your dough. When the cycle has ended, shape the dough and place in an oiled 9"x5" loaf pan. Let rise until double in bulk. Bake at 350 degrees for 25 to 30 minutes. Serves 8.

Rhonda Reeder
Ellicott City, MD

Whole-Wheat Bread

4 c. milk
¼ c. sugar
4 t. salt
1 env. active dry yeast

5 c. whole-wheat flour
2 T. shortening
5 c. all-purpose flour

Heat milk slowly in a small saucepan over medium heat until tiny bubbles appear around the edges. Remove from heat and add sugar and salt; stir and cool to lukewarm. Add yeast. Combine yeast mixture with whole-wheat flour in the bowl of a heavy-duty mixer, beating thoroughly until bubbles are formed. Beat in shortening. Beat in enough all-purpose flour to form a dough that clears the sides of the bowl. Turn out into a well-floured bowl. Let rest 10 minutes. Knead until smooth, elastic and satiny. Place in a greased bowl. Cover and let rise in a warm place until double in bulk. Punch down dough. Let rise again until double in bulk. Divide into 4 equal portions. Round each into a smooth ball, cover well and let rest 10 to 15 minutes. Mold into loaves. Place in greased 9"x5" loaf pans and let rise until double in bulk. Bake at 375 degrees for 40 to 45 minutes. Makes 4 one-pound loaves; serves 8.

Jane Ramicone
Berea, OH

homemade yumminess

The kids can make homemade butter in no time… wonderful on still-warm slices of bread! Just fill a jar with heavy cream, add a tight-fitting lid and roll and shake until the butter forms!

Old-World Black Bread

3¾ c. rye flour
3¾ c. all-purpose flour
2 env. active dry yeast
½ c. warm water (110 to
  115 degrees)
½ c. baking cocoa
¼ c. sugar

2 T. caraway seeds
2 t. salt
2 t. instant coffee granules
2 c. water
¼ c. vinegar
¼ c. corn syrup
¼ c. butter

Combine flours in a large bowl; reserve 3 cups flour mixture in another large bowl. Sprinkle yeast over warm water in a small bowl and stir until dissolved; set aside. Stir cocoa, sugar, caraway seeds, salt and instant coffee into 3 cups reserved flour mixture. Combine water, vinegar, corn syrup and butter in a medium saucepan over low heat. Heat just until warm; butter does not need to be completely melted. Add to cocoa mixture and blend well. Add dissolved yeast and stir until thoroughly combined. Stir in enough additional flour mixture, one cup at a time, until dough no longer clings to sides of bowl. Turn out onto a lightly floured surface; cover and let rest 10 minutes. Knead dough until smooth and elastic, about 15 minutes. Place in a greased bowl and turn greased side up. Cover and let rise in a warm place about one hour, or until double in bulk. Punch dough down and turn out onto a lightly floured surface. Divide dough in half; shape each portion into a smooth ball. Place each portion in the center of a greased 8" round cake pan. Cover and let rise in a warm place about one hour, or until double in bulk. Bake at 350 degrees for 45 to 50 minutes, until loaves sound hollow when tapped lightly. Remove from pans and place on wire racks. Makes 2 loaves; serves 8.

Sharon Stellrecht
Camano Island, WA

"When I was an exchange student in Germany, my German 'mother' baked delicious Russian-German bread. I couldn't ask her for the recipe due to the language barrier, but years later I found this recipe, which is very similar."

—Sharon

Focaccia

Perfect served with pasta! Try dipping warm slices of focaccia in pesto, marinara sauce or roasted garlic…yummy!

4 to 4½ c. all-purpose flour, divided
1 env. instant yeast
1 T. dried basil
1 t. dried thyme
2 cloves garlic, pressed
½ t. salt
1½ c. warm water (110 to 115 degrees)
1 t. honey
2 T. olive oil, divided

Stir together 2 cups flour, yeast, basil, thyme, garlic and salt in a large bowl. Combine warm water and honey in a small bowl; blend into flour mixture. Add enough remaining flour until dough is smooth and not sticky; knead on a lightly floured surface 8 to 10 minutes. Cover and let rise until double in bulk. Spread one tablespoon oil on a baking sheet and transfer dough to baking sheet; pat into a 14"x10" rectangle. Brush dough with remaining olive oil; let rise 5 minutes. Bake at 375 degrees for 30 minutes, or until golden. Serves 10.

Elizabeth Romaine
Columbus, OH

Mediterranean Loaf

3 c. bread flour
2 T. sugar
2 t. instant yeast
2 t. salt
½ c. black olives, chopped

4 T. olive oil, divided
1¼ c. warm water (110 to
   115 degrees)
¼ c. cornmeal

Sift together flour, sugar, yeast and salt in a large bowl. Stir in black olives, 3 tablespoons olive oil and warm water. Place dough on a floured surface and knead 10 minutes. Cover and let rise until double in bulk. Punch down and knead again 5 minutes. Let rise again until double in bulk. Place a 13"x9" baking pan of water on the bottom rack of the oven and turn oven to 500 degrees. Spread remaining olive oil on a baking sheet; sprinkle with cornmeal. Shape dough into a round loaf and place on baking sheet. Bake at 500 degrees for 15 minutes; reduce oven temperature to 375 degrees and bake another 20 to 30 minutes. Serves 10.

Darrell Lawry
Kissimmee, FL

tasty twist

Try using green olives to give the bread a different flavor.

Pesto Marbled Bread

1 env. active dry yeast
1 t. sugar
2 c. warm water (110 to
   115 degrees)
2 c. bread flour

1 T. salt
3 T. olive oil
3 c. all-purpose flour, divided
6 T. pesto

Stir yeast and sugar into warm water in a bowl; set aside 5 minutes. Stir in bread flour, salt and oil; mix until smooth. Stir in 2 cups flour and knead on a floured surface 10 minutes. Add enough flour until dough is no longer sticky. Place dough in an oiled bowl. Cover and let rise until double in bulk. Divide dough in half and roll each half into an 11"x7" rectangle. Spread pesto evenly in the center of each rectangle and roll up jelly-roll style, pinching ends to seal. Place, seam-side down, on an oiled baking sheet; cover and let rise until double in bulk. Bake at 350 degrees for 35 minutes. Serves 16.

Mary Murray
Gooseberry Patch

Dilly Bread

Great for sandwiches or spread with cream cheese and sprinkled with chives.

tasty twist

Toast a slice of Dilly Bread and top it with cream cheese and smoked salmon.

1 env. active dry yeast
¼ c. warm water (110 to 115 degrees)
1 c. cottage cheese
2 T. sugar
1 T. onion, minced
2 T. butter

2½ t. dill weed
1 t. salt
¼ t. baking soda
1 egg, beaten
2¼ to 2½ c. all-purpose flour
2 T. butter, melted
1 T. coarse salt

Sprinkle yeast over warm water in a small bowl; set aside. Heat cottage cheese just until warm; place in a mixing bowl. Stir in sugar, onion, 2 tablespoons butter, dill weed, salt, baking soda, egg and yeast mixture; add flour to form a stiff dough. Knead several times on a lightly floured surface; cover and let dough rise until double in bulk. Punch down; divide into 2 loaves. Place each in a greased one-pound coffee can; let rise again until double in bulk. Brush tops of loaves with melted butter and sprinkle with coarse salt; bake at 350 degrees for 30 to 35 minutes. Makes 2 loaves; serves 16.

Irene Senne
Aplington, IA

Cheddar Quick Bread

3½ c. biscuit baking mix
2½ c. shredded sharp Cheddar cheese
1 t. garlic salt

⅓ c. fresh chives, chopped
2 eggs
1¼ c. milk

Combine biscuit mix, cheese, garlic salt and chives in a large mixing bowl; set aside. Beat eggs and milk in another mixing bowl; stir into cheese mixture just until moistened. Pour into 4 greased and floured 5"x3" loaf pans; bake at 350 degrees for 35 to 40 minutes. Cool 10 minutes; remove from pans. Slice and serve warm. Makes 4 mini loaves. Serves 8.

Lori Burris
Gooseberry Patch

Dilly Bread

Quick Sourdough Bread

3 T. instant mashed potato flakes
¾ c. sugar
2½ c. warm water (110 to 115 degrees), divided
1 env. active dry yeast
½ c. plus 2 T. oil, divided
1 T. salt
6 to 7 c. bread flour
2 T. butter, melted

Mix potato flakes, sugar, one cup warm water and yeast in a large bowl. Cover and let stand overnight at room temperature. In the morning, combine ½ cup oil, salt, remaining 1½ cups warm water and flour in a large bowl; stir into yeast mixture. Cover and let dough rise until double in bulk; punch down and divide into thirds. Knead each third 6 to 8 times; shape into loaves. Place each loaf in a greased 8"x4" loaf pan; brush tops of loaves with remaining oil. Let rise until double in bulk; bake at 350 degrees for 25 to 30 minutes. Remove from oven and brush tops with melted butter. Makes 3 loaves; serves 12.

Theone Neel
Bastian, VA

Granny's Country Cornbread

1¼ c. cornmeal
¾ c. all-purpose flour
5 T. sugar
2 t. baking powder
½ t. salt
1 c. buttermilk
⅓ c. oil
1 egg, beaten
1 c. shredded Cheddar cheese
1 c. corn
1 T. jalapeño pepper, minced

Mix together cornmeal, flour, sugar, baking powder and salt in a large bowl. Make a well in center; pour in buttermilk, oil and egg. Stir just until ingredients are lightly moistened. Fold in cheese, corn and jalapeño; pour into a greased 8" cast-iron skillet. Bake at 375 degrees for 20 minutes, or until a toothpick inserted in the center comes out clean. Let cool slightly; cut into wedges. Serves 4 to 6.

Rachel Anderson
Livermore, CA

Spoonbread

A yummy Southern-style cornbread recipe.

2 eggs, beaten
8½-oz. pkg. corn muffin mix
12-oz. can creamed corn
12-oz. can corn, drained

¼ c. margarine, melted
1 c. sour cream
1 c. shredded Cheddar cheese

Combine all ingredients except cheese in a large bowl; stir well. Spread in a lightly buttered 11"x7" baking pan; bake at 350 degrees for 35 minutes. Sprinkle cheese on top; return to oven until cheese is melted. Serves 6.

Cha McCarl
Enid, OK

Just Peachy Bread
Pudding, page 190

bread puddings + custards

Grab a spoon and dive into these luscious custards and bread puddings. From Chocolate Lover's Bread Pudding to Brownie Pudding Trifle to Lemon Pudding, your sweet tooth is covered.

Lemony Bread Pudding

A yummy comfort food topped with lemon sauce.

2 c. dry bread, cubed
4 c. milk, scalded
3 T. butter, divided
¼ t. plus ⅛ t. salt, divided
1¼ c. sugar, divided
4 eggs, beaten

1 t. vanilla extract
1 T. cornstarch
⅛ t. nutmeg
1 c. boiling water
1½ T. lemon juice

Soak bread in hot milk 5 minutes. Add one tablespoon butter, ¼ teaspoon salt and ¾ cup sugar. Place eggs in a large bowl. Pour bread mixture over eggs, add vanilla and mix well. Spoon into a greased 2-quart casserole dish or individual ramekins. Set casserole dish or ramekins in a larger pan filled with hot water and bake at 350 degrees for 50 minutes for casserole dish or for 30 minutes for ramekins, or until firm. Mix remaining sugar, cornstarch, remaining salt and nutmeg in a small saucepan; gradually add boiling water. Cook over low heat until thick and clear. Add remaining butter and lemon juice; blend thoroughly. Serve over bread pudding. Serves 6.

Linda Staley
Ashley, OH

Creamy Pear Bread Pudding

1 t. rum extract
1 t. water
½ c. raisins
1 T. butter
2 c. pears, peeled, cored and
  sliced

½ c. sugar, divided
4 c. white bread, torn
3 c. milk, scalded
3 eggs, beaten
1 t. vanilla extract
1 c. whipping cream

Blend together rum extract and water in a small saucepan. Heat just to boiling and pour over raisins in a small bowl. Melt butter in saucepan over medium heat; stir in pear slices and sauté 4 minutes. Stir in ¼ cup sugar and continue to cook 2 minutes. Place bread in a buttered 2-quart casserole dish, pour in milk and let soak 5 minutes. Fold in raisin and pear mixtures. Thoroughly combine eggs, remaining sugar, vanilla and cream in a small bowl; combine with bread mixture. Bake at 350 degrees for 50 minutes. Serves 6.

Tori Willis
Champaign, IL

"Pears and bread pudding are two of my favorites…so I came up with this recipe that combines the best of both!"

—Tori

any bread will do

Substitute any bread, such as brioche or challah, in this recipe.

Cinnamon Bread Pudding

The cinnamon bread makes this pudding extra special, and the warm butter sauce is so good drizzled over the top!

6 eggs

2 c. milk

2 c. half-and-half, divided

1 c. sugar

2 t. vanilla extract

6 c. cinnamon bread, cubed

½ c. brown sugar, packed

¼ c. butter

½ c. corn syrup

Whisk eggs in a large mixing bowl; blend in milk, 1¾ cups half-and-half, sugar and vanilla until combined. Stir in bread cubes until lightly moistened. Spread mixture evenly in a greased 2-quart casserole dish. Bake at 325 degrees for 55 to 60 minutes, until center starts to firm. Heat brown sugar and butter in a small saucepan over medium-low heat until butter is melted. Carefully add corn syrup and remaining half-and-half. Cook, stirring constantly, one to 2 minutes, until sugar dissolves and mixture is smooth. Serve over warm pudding. Serves 6.

Sharon Gould
Howard City, MI

kitchen tip

Don't let the bread cubes soak too long or your bread pudding will be too mushy.

Chocolate Lover's Bread Pudding

4 slices bread, crusts removed

1 1-oz. sq. unsweetened baking chocolate, chopped

4 c. milk

2 eggs, beaten

1 c. sugar

1 t. vanilla extract

Garnish: whipped cream

Tear bread into bite-size pieces and place in a small saucepan. Stir in chocolate and milk and bring to a boil, stirring constantly. Remove from heat. Blend eggs and sugar together in a bowl; gradually pour milk mixture over eggs, stirring constantly. Mix in vanilla and pour into a greased 2-quart casserole dish. Place casserole dish in a larger pan filled with water. Bake at 350 degrees for one hour, or until a knife inserted in the center comes out clean. Top servings with whipped cream. Serves 6.

Jo Ann
Gooseberry Patch

Chocolate Lover's
Bread Pudding

Just Peachy Bread Pudding

1 loaf French bread, cubed	12-oz. can evaporated milk
16-oz. can sliced peaches, drained	2 c. milk
½ c. raisins	½ t. cinnamon
4 eggs, separated and divided	¼ t. nutmeg
¾ c. sugar	1 t. coconut extract
	1 T. vanilla extract

Fill a buttered 3-quart casserole dish with bread cubes, peach slices and raisins; stir gently and set aside. Combine 2 eggs and 2 egg whites with sugar in a small bowl, reserving remaining yolks for another use. Stir together evaporated milk, milk, spices, coconut and vanilla extracts and egg mixture in a bowl; blend. Pour egg mixture evenly over bread, gently stirring to coat. Bake at 350 degrees for 30 to 40 minutes, until a knife inserted near the center comes out clean. Serves 8.

Erin Doell
Glen Ellyn, IL

Texas-Style Bread Pudding

2 T. butter	2 eggs, beaten
6 slices bread	⅔ c. sugar
2 Red Delicious or Cortland apples, peeled and chopped	1½ c. whipping cream
3 T. raisins	1 c. apple cider
¼ c. walnuts, chopped	1½ t. cinnamon
	½ t. nutmeg

Butter one side of each bread slice and cut diagonally into 4 pieces. Lay 8 bread pieces in bottom of ungreased 2-quart casserole dish. Divide apples into 4 equal amounts, then alternate layers of apples, then bread; repeat 2 times. Toss together raisins and walnuts and place over bread layer. Top with remaining apple pieces. Blend eggs and sugar in a bowl; stir in cream, apple cider, cinnamon and nutmeg. Pour over top of bread mixture. Cover and bake at 350 degrees for 40 to 50 minutes. Serves 6.

Corrine Lane
Gooseberry Patch

Tropical Pineapple Pudding

Teresa Sullivan (Westerville, OH)

I like to serve this as a side whenever I make ham for dinner.

½ c. margarine, melted
5 slices white bread, cubed
3 eggs, beaten
3 T. all-purpose flour

½ t. salt
¾ c. sugar
20-oz. can crushed pineapple,
    undrained

Melt margarine in a large skillet over medium heat; add bread cubes and sauté until golden; set aside. Place eggs in a large bowl and add flour, salt, sugar and pineapple; mix well. Pour mixture into a greased 1½-quart casserole dish. Add bread cubes, pushing bread down into pineapple mixture. Bake at 350 degrees for 35 to 40 minutes. Serves 6.

French Apple Bread Pudding

Topped with whipped cream, this is terrific!

3 eggs, beaten
12-oz. can sweetened
    condensed milk
3 apples, peeled, cored and
    chopped
1¾ c. hot water

¼ c. butter, melted
1 t. cinnamon
1 t. vanilla extract
4 c. French bread, cubed
½ c. raisins
Garnish: whipped cream

Combine eggs, milk, apples, water, butter, cinnamon and vanilla in a large bowl. Stir in bread and raisins, completely moistening bread. Turn into a greased 9"x9" baking pan. Bake at 350 degrees for one hour. Garnish with whipped cream. Serves 8.

Bonnie Stanley
Clintwood, VA

Old-Fashioned Chocolate Pudding

"Made from scratch, this is my mother-in-law's recipe for a homemade treat the whole family loves."
—Michelle

¾ c. sugar
1 T. baking cocoa
2 T. all-purpose flour

2 c. milk
1 t. vanilla extract
Garnish: whipped topping

Combine all ingredients except garnish in a heavy saucepan over medium heat, stirring constantly; bring to a rolling boil and stir until thickened. Remove from heat; cool. Garnish each serving with a spoonful of whipped topping. Serves 4.

Michelle Urdahl
Litchfield, MN

Mocha-Chocolate Steamed Pudding

Don't be intimidated by steamed puddings…they're delicious and surprisingly easy to make. Family & friends will be amazed!

4 1-oz. sqs. unsweetened baking chocolate
¾ c. milk
2 T. instant coffee granules
½ c. butter, softened
1 c. sugar

2 eggs, separated
1 t. vanilla extract
1¼ c. all-purpose flour
1 t. baking powder
¼ t. salt

Melt chocolate in a double boiler over medium-low heat; stir until smooth. Set aside to cool. Heat milk and instant coffee in a small saucepan until milk is warm and coffee has dissolved completely; set aside to cool. Combine butter and sugar in a large bowl; blend until creamy. Add 2 egg yolks and vanilla; blend well. Combine flour, baking powder and salt in a small bowl; set aside. After milk mixture has cooled completely, blend into butter mixture alternately with flour mixture. Add the cooled chocolate. In a small bowl, beat egg whites until soft peaks form; stir a small amount of the beaten egg whites into the pudding batter. Carefully fold in remaining egg whites. Pour batter into a steamed pudding mold that has been coated with non-stick vegetable spray. Cover with lid and set mold on a trivet inside a large stockpot. Pour in boiling water until water comes halfway up pudding mold. Cover stockpot and place over medium-low heat. Keep water at a low simmer for 3½ hours; add water as necessary to maintain water level. Remove mold and let stand covered 15 minutes to cool. Remove lid and turn pudding out onto a serving dish to cool completely. Pudding will keep for up to one week in refrigerator. Serves 8 to 10.

Sharron Tillman
Hampton, VA

Maple Bread Pudding

Nothing ends a meal quite like old-fashioned bread pudding.

4 c. French bread, cubed
1 c. raisins
¼ c. chopped pecans
4 eggs
½ c. sugar
⅛ t. nutmeg

2 c. milk
½ c. maple syrup
Garnish: whipped topping, maple syrup and pecan halves

Spread bread cubes in a greased 8"x8" baking pan; sprinkle with raisins and pecans. Beat eggs in a mixing bowl; add sugar, nutmeg, milk and syrup. Pour evenly over bread mixture; bake at 350 degrees for one hour, or until a knife inserted in the center comes out clean. To serve, spoon warm pudding into individual dessert bowls and top each serving with a dollop of whipped topping. Drizzle tops with maple syrup and sprinkle with pecan halves. Serves 6.

Joan Barton
Goffstown, NH

Granny Christian's Biscuit Pudding

"My grandmother, who was born in 1900, made the best biscuit pudding I've ever eaten! After misplacing her recipe, and finally retrieving it, I am happy to share it here."

—Linda

15 frozen biscuits, thawed
3 c. milk
1½ c. water
2 eggs, beaten

1 T. vanilla extract
¾ c. butter
½ c. sugar

Bake biscuits according to package directions. Cool and crumble; set aside. Mix together remaining ingredients except butter and sugar in a large bowl; add crumbled biscuits. Pour into a lightly greased 13"x9" baking pan. Bake at 350 degrees for 45 minutes; remove from oven and set aside. Melt butter in a saucepan over medium heat; add sugar and cook until sugar is dissolved. Pour over pudding. Serves 10 to 12.

Linda Stone
Cookeville, TN

English Bread Pudding

10 slices day-old bread, torn
½ c. shortening
½ c. sugar
1½ c. golden raisins

apple pie spice to taste
Optional: custard or whipping cream

"This recipe is made with leftover bread. It was handed down to me from my mum, and everybody loves it!"

—Karen

Place bread in a large bowl. Cover with cold water; let stand 30 minutes. Drain; squeeze water from bread and return to bowl. Add shortening and sugar; mix well. Add raisins and spice; mix thoroughly. Place in a lightly greased 2-quart casserole dish. Bake at 350 degrees for one hour. Serve warm or cold; garnish as desired. Serves 8 to 10.

Karen Foster
Hampshire, England

Old-Fashioned Bread Pudding

When the weather is cold outside, nothing brings the family in faster than the aroma of bread pudding baking in the oven.

kitchen tip

Fresh whipped cream is oh-so easy to make. Combine one cup heavy cream with ¼ cup powdered sugar and one teaspoon vanilla extract in a chilled bowl. Beat with chilled beaters until stiff peaks form. Dollop onto a big slice of cake or pie…yummy!

10 slices white bread, cubed
¼ c. butter, melted
½ c. raisins
1 t. cinnamon
¾ c. sugar
6 eggs, beaten
2 t. vanilla extract
½ t. salt
3 c. milk
⅛ t. nutmeg
Garnish: whipped topping

Combine bread cubes, butter, raisins and cinnamon in a large bowl. Mix well; spread in a lightly greased 2-quart casserole dish. Blend together sugar, eggs, vanilla and salt in a medium bowl until sugar is dissolved. Add milk; beat well. Pour over bread mixture; let stand 5 minutes. Sprinkle with nutmeg. Bake at 375 degrees for 25 minutes. Cool slightly before serving. Garnish with dollops of whipped topping. Serves 8.

Charlene McCain
Bakersfield, CA

Raisin Bread Pudding

When it comes to comfort food, this is the best!

½ loaf white bread, torn
6 c. milk
5 eggs, beaten
1 T. cinnamon
1½ c. brown sugar, packed
1 c. raisins

cinnamon and sugar to taste
1 c. sugar
2 T. cornstarch
2 c. boiling water
2 t. vanilla extract
¼ c. butter

Place bread in a greased 13"x9" baking pan. Blend milk, eggs, cinnamon, brown sugar and raisins in a large bowl. Mix well and pour over bread; sprinkle with a mixture of cinnamon and sugar. Bake at 350 degrees for 1½ to 2 hours, until golden brown. Combine sugar and cornstarch in a saucepan. Gradually stir in boiling water, bring to a boil and continue boiling one minute, stirring constantly. Add vanilla and butter, stirring until butter is melted. Pour vanilla sauce over slices of cooled bread pudding. Serves 10.

Janice Roebuck
North Judson, IN

Grandpa's Bread Pudding

2 eggs, beaten
1 c. sugar
2 c. milk
1 t. vanilla extract
10 slices bread, torn and
   divided

16-oz. can fruit cocktail,
   drained
2 T. butter, melted
Garnish: cinnamon

Mix together eggs, sugar, milk and vanilla in a bowl; set aside. Arrange half the bread in a greased 9"x5" loaf pan. Pour fruit over top; cover with remaining bread. Pour egg mixture over top; drizzle with butter and sprinkle with cinnamon. Bake at 350 degrees for 50 minutes. Serves 10 to 12.

Carolyn Helewski
Arcadia, FL

"Everyone loves this bread pudding! It's so simple to put together, and the fruit cocktail is a delicious, unexpected touch."

—Carolyn

Favorite Vanilla Pudding Mix

1¼ c. powdered milk	½ t. salt
1½ c. sugar	1¼ c. cornstarch
¼ t. nutmeg	½ t. vanilla powder

Combine all ingredients; store in an airtight container. Attach a gift tag with instructions. Makes 4 cups.

Instructions:

Mix ½ cup mix with 2 cups milk in a saucepan. Bring mixture to a boil, stirring constantly; reduce heat and simmer until thickened, continuing to stir constantly. Remove from heat. Pour pudding into individual serving dishes; refrigerate until chilled. Serves 4 to 6.

tasty twist

Want to switch it up? Leave out the nutmeg and substitute any extract in place of vanilla when cooking...lemon, banana and pineapple are all delicious!

Family-Style Chocolate Pudding Mix

For a mocha flavor, add one teaspoon instant coffee granules to the mix.

2½ c. powdered milk	1½ c. baking cocoa
3 c. cornstarch	1½ t. salt
5 c. sugar	

Combine all ingredients; store in an airtight container. Attach a gift tag with instructions. Makes 12 cups.

Instructions:

Shake mix before using; measure out ⅔ cup mix and place in a saucepan. Add 2 cups milk; heat over low heat. Stir until mixture thickens and boils; continue stirring for one minute. Remove from heat; pour into individual serving dishes. Refrigerate until chilled. Serves 10.

Favorite Vanilla
Pudding Mix

Hot Cinnamon
Pudding

Hot Cinnamon Pudding

2 c. brown sugar, packed
1½ c. cold water
¼ c. butter, melted and divided
¾ c. sugar
1 c. milk
2 c. all-purpose flour
2 t. baking powder
2 t. cinnamon
¼ t. salt
Optional: chopped nuts
Garnish: whipped cream or
    vanilla ice cream

    Mix together brown sugar, water and 2 tablespoons butter in a bowl. Pour into a greased and floured 1½-quart casserole dish. Mix together remaining ingredients except nuts and garnish in a bowl. Pour over brown sugar mixture. Top with nuts, if desired. Bake at 350 degrees for 45 minutes. Garnish as desired; serve warm. Serves 6.

Jennie Wiseman
Coshocton, OH

"When my girls were little, they would sled down a tiny hill in front of our home with their dad. When they came back in, they warmed up with this cozy pudding."

—Jennie

Slow-Cooker Tapioca Pudding

8 c. milk
1 c. small pearl tapioca,
    uncooked
1 to 1½ c. sugar
4 eggs, beaten
1 t. vanilla extract
½ t. almond extract
Garnish: whipped cream,
    sliced fresh fruit

    Add milk, tapioca and sugar to a slow cooker; stir gently. Cover and cook on high setting for 3 hours. Mix together eggs, extracts and 2 spoonfuls of hot mixture from slow cooker in a bowl. Slowly stir mixture into slow cooker. Cover and cook on high setting for an additional 20 minutes. Chill overnight. Garnish as desired. Serves 10 to 12.

Leisha Howard
Seattle, WA

Upside-Down Date Pudding

Try this tasty upside-down version of an old-fashioned dessert.

tasty twist

Swap out walnuts for pecans.

1 c. chopped dates
2½ c. boiling water, divided
½ c. sugar
2 c. brown sugar, firmly
  packed and divided
3 T. butter, divided
1 egg

1½ c. all-purpose flour
1 t. baking soda
½ t. baking powder
½ t. salt
1 c. chopped walnuts
Garnish: sweetened whipped
  cream

Combine dates and one cup boiling water in a small bowl; set aside. Combine sugar, ½ cup brown sugar, 2 tablespoons butter and egg in a large mixing bowl; beat with an electric mixer at medium speed until blended. Combine flour, baking soda, baking powder and salt in a separate bowl; stir well. Add to sugar mixture, beating well until a crumbly mixture forms. Stir in nuts and cooled date mixture. Spoon batter into a lightly greased 13"x9" baking pan. Combine remaining brown sugar, remaining boiling water and remaining butter in a bowl, stirring well. Pour brown sugar mixture evenly over batter. Bake at 375 degrees for 35 to 40 minutes. Cut into squares and invert onto serving plates. Serve warm with whipped cream. Serves 12.

Beth Cavanaugh
Gooseberry Patch

Bragging-Rights Banana Pudding

5¼-oz. pkg. instant vanilla
   pudding mix
3 c. milk
16-oz. container sour cream
12-oz. container frozen
   whipped topping, thawed

10-oz. pkg. vanilla wafers,
   divided
4 bananas, sliced and divided

"This recipe was handed down from my wonderful mother-in-law. It is the ultimate crowd-pleaser!"

—Mary

Beat dry pudding mix and milk in a bowl with an electric mixer at low speed 2 to 3 minutes, until thickened. Beat in sour cream; fold in topping. Set aside several vanilla wafers. Layer half each of remaining wafers, bananas and pudding mixture in a large deep bowl. Repeat layers. Crush reserved wafers and sprinkle on top. Cover; chill until serving time. Serves 10 to 15.

Mary Jackson
Fishers, IN

reunion recipes

Before your next family reunion, ask everyone to bring their favorite baking recipe, as well as any stories about the recipe. Perhaps it's been handed down for generations, or maybe a tasty dish was created by accident. Retype the recipes and stories, then make plenty of copies to share at the next reunion!

Black Bottom Pudding
Marty Darling (Coshocton, OH)

1 c. all-purpose flour
1¼ c. sugar, divided
2 t. baking powder
¼ t. salt
½ c. milk
2 T. butter, melted

7 T. baking cocoa, divided
1 egg
½ c. brown sugar, packed
1½ c. boiling water
Garnish: whipped cream

Sift together flour, ¾ cup sugar, baking powder and salt in a bowl. Add milk, butter, 3 tablespoons cocoa and egg. Mix together; pour into a greased 8"x8" baking pan. Mix together remaining sugar, brown sugar and remaining cocoa in a bowl. Sprinkle over mixture in pan. Carefully pour boiling water over all; do not stir. Bake at 375 degrees for 35 to 40 minutes. Cool, cut and serve upside down with whipped cream. Serves 6.

Raisin Bread Pudding + Vanilla Sauce

A slow-cooker version of a classic dessert.

8 slices bread, cubed
4 eggs
2 c. milk
½ c. sugar

¼ c. butter, melted
¼ c. raisins
½ t. cinnamon

kitchen tip

Look for a slow cooker that's at least 4 quarts in size.

Place bread cubes in a greased slow cooker and set aside. Whisk together eggs and milk in a bowl; stir in remaining ingredients. Pour over bread cubes and stir. Cover and cook on high setting for one hour. Reduce setting to low; cook an additional 3 to 4 hours. Serve warm with Vanilla Sauce. Serves 6.

Vanilla Sauce

2 T. butter
2 T. all-purpose flour
1 c. water

¾ c. sugar
1 t. vanilla extract

Melt butter in a small saucepan over medium heat; stir in flour until smooth. Gradually add water, sugar and vanilla. Bring to a boil; cook and stir 2 minutes, or until thickened. Keep warm.

Jo Ann
Gooseberry Patch

Christmas Date Pudding

Serve this special pudding for any occasion.

1 c. dates, chopped	1 t. baking powder
¾ c. boiling water	1 t. baking soda
1 c. sugar	salt to taste
1 egg, beaten	½ c. chopped nuts
1 T. butter, melted	1 t. vanilla extract
1½ c. all-purpose flour	Garnish: whipped cream

Mix dates and boiling water in a large bowl and let stand 10 minutes. Do not drain water. Mix sugar, egg and butter in a small bowl; add to dates. Combine flour, baking powder, baking soda, salt and nuts in a bowl and add to date mixture. Add vanilla. Pour into a greased and floured 13"x9" baking pan. Bake at 350 degrees for 35 to 45 minutes. Cool and serve with whipped cream. Serves 10.

Sally Davis
Payne, OH

light dusting
Dust with powdered sugar so it looks like snow.

Christmas Plum Pudding

Prepare two weeks before Christmas Day. Begin by soaking the dates and raisins the night before you want to make the pudding.

2 c. all-purpose flour
1 t. baking soda
1 t. cinnamon
½ t. nutmeg
½ t. salt
1 c. butter, softened
1 c. dark brown sugar

½ c. molasses
3 eggs
¼ c. milk
¼ c. slivered almonds
⅔ c. flaked coconut
1 c. plain bread crumbs

Sift together flour, baking soda, cinnamon, nutmeg and salt in a bowl; set aside. Blend together butter and brown sugar in a large bowl. Add molasses and eggs; beat in flour mixture and milk alternately. Stir in Date-Raisin Mixture, almonds, coconut and bread crumbs. Pour into a greased 6-cup mold. Cover with buttered wax paper, tie with string and cover again with aluminum foil. Place on a rack in a large stockpot or Dutch oven. Add water to just below rack. Cover and steam over medium-low heat 3 hours. Keep adding water to pan so it does not go dry. Cool and store pudding in covered mold at room temperature until Christmas Day. To serve, steam 2 hours over medium-low heat; remove from heat and cool 10 minutes. Loosen edges and invert onto a serving plate. Decorate with holly and serve with Brandy Butter. Serves 10.

Date-Raisin Mixture

½ c. dates, chopped
½ c. golden raisins

½ c. brandy

Soak dates and raisins in brandy in a bowl the night before making the pudding.

Brandy Butter

1 c. powdered sugar
½ c. butter, softened

1 T. brandy
1 T. rum

Beat powdered sugar and butter in a bowl. Beat in brandy and rum; chill.

Lemon Pudding

"This light dessert recipe has been in the family for years. The sweet-tart taste makes a great ending to any meal."

—Dorothy

1 c. sugar
2 T. butter, softened
2 T. all-purpose flour

zest and juice of 1½ lemons
2 eggs, separated
1 c. milk

Blend sugar and butter in a mixing bowl; mix in flour. Add lemon zest and juice; blend well. Mix in egg yolks and milk; set aside. Whip egg whites in a bowl until stiff peaks form; fold in lemon mixture. Pour into a buttered one-quart casserole dish; set in a shallow baking pan filled with ½ inch water. Bake at 350 degrees for 35 minutes. Serves 6.

Dorothy Baldauf
Crystal Lake, IL

Delicious Custard Cake Pudding

1 lb. leftover tea bread or scones

¼ c. butter

2 tart apples, peeled and sliced

4 oz. dates, chopped, or 4 oz. dried cranberries

8 whole eggs plus 4 yolks

⅔ c. sugar

½ t. salt

½ t. nutmeg

⅛ c. rum

1½ qts. milk

1¼ c. whipping cream

powdered sugar

whipped cream

2 10-oz. pkgs. frozen raspberries or strawberries

2 T. cornstarch

¼ c. raspberry syrup

Crumble bread or scones and spread in bottom of a greased 2-quart casserole dish. Dot with butter. Arrange sliced apples over the bread and add dates or cranberries to the top. To eggs, add sugar, salt, nutmeg and rum. Beat until well combined. Combine milk and cream in a saucepan; heat to boiling, then scald, watching for foaming. Carefully add hot milk to egg mixture and stir. Pour over contents in the casserole dish. Add hot water to a roasting pan; place pudding dish in one inch of water in pan. Bake at 375 degrees for 45 minutes, or until knife inserted in the center comes out clean. When done, remove dish and top with powdered sugar and whipped cream to taste. Thaw and crush raspberries. Put cornstarch in a microwave-safe bowl and add raspberry syrup. Microwave on high 30 seconds, stirring the cornstarch so there are no lumps. Add to thawed berries; heat until the sauce is slightly thickened. Top individual servings of pudding with approximately 2 tablespoons of raspberry sauce. Serves 20.

Brownie Pudding Trifle

Brownie Pudding Trifle

Use your prettiest cut-glass bowl for this luscious layered dessert.

20-oz. pkg. brownie mix
3.9-oz. pkg. instant chocolate
  pudding mix
14-oz. can sweetened
  condensed milk
½ c. water
16-oz. container frozen
  whipped topping, thawed
  and divided

Bake brownie mix according to package directions. Cool completely; cut into one-inch squares and set aside. Combine pudding mix, condensed milk and water in a large bowl; stir until smooth. Fold in 3 cups whipped topping. Layer half the brownies, half the pudding mixture and half the remaining whipped topping in a glass serving bowl. Repeat layering. Chill 8 hours or overnight before serving. Serves 12.

Anna McMaster
Portland, OR

Baked Custard

Creamy and comforting…top with a dollop of whipped cream and a dash of nutmeg.

1 c. evaporated milk
1 c. water
4 egg yolks
⅓ c. sugar
¼ t. salt
½ t. vanilla extract

Combine milk and water in a saucepan; heat just to boiling and set aside. Beat yolks slightly in a bowl; add sugar, salt and vanilla. Gradually add hot milk mixture to egg mixture, stirring constantly. Divide among 4 greased custard cups; set in a pan of hot water. Bake at 325 degrees for 50 minutes, or until a knife inserted in the center comes out clean. Serve warm or chilled. Serves 4.

Stephanie Mayer
Portsmouth, VA

Rose's Baked Custard

A simple dessert like Grandma used to make.

1 egg	¾ t. vanilla extract
1 c. milk	⅛ t. salt
3 T. sugar	⅛ t. nutmeg

Beat egg in a small bowl; stir in milk, sugar, vanilla and salt. Pour into 2 ungreased 6-ounce custard cups. Sprinkle with nutmeg. Set custard cups in a baking pan filled with ½ inch hot water. Bake at 350 degrees for 35 minutes, or until set. Serves 2.

Rose Jones
Champaign, IL

Miss Piggy Pudding

"When we visited my husband's grandmother, she almost always had this dessert ready for us. Many years later, I served this to a couple of young men far from home. One of them exclaimed with tears in his eyes, 'Miss Piggy Pudding... just like my mom used to make!' and the name stuck."

—Kathy

½ c. butter, softened	3.9-oz. pkg. instant chocolate pudding mix
1 c. all-purpose flour	
Optional: 1 c. chopped nuts	3.4-oz. pkg. instant vanilla pudding mix
8-oz. pkg. cream cheese, softened	
1 c. powdered sugar	3 c. milk
8-oz. container frozen whipped topping, thawed and divided	Garnish: chopped nuts, chocolate candy sprinkles

Mix together butter, flour and nuts, if using, in a bowl. Pat into an ungreased 13"x9" baking pan. Bake at 350 degrees for 20 minutes; cool. Beat together cream cheese and powdered sugar in a bowl until smooth. Blend in one cup whipped topping; spread over baked crust and set aside. Combine pudding mixes and milk in a bowl. Let stand until slightly thickened; pour over cream cheese mixture. Refrigerate until completely set. Spread with remaining whipped topping; sprinkle with chopped nuts and sprinkles, if desired. Chill until ready to serve. Serves 10 to 12.

Kathy Sharp
Westerville, OH

Miss Piggy Pudding

Butter-Pecan Ice
Cream, page 237

frozen treats

Who needs an ice cream truck when you've got icy treats like these? Make room in your freezer for delicious delights like Rainbow Sherbet Cake, Snowballs and Banana Split Ice Cream! You will have the kids lined up and patiently waiting for these treats.

Rainbow Sherbet Cake

Delightfully light and creamy.

1 prepared angel food cake
1 pt. orange sherbet, softened
1 pt. raspberry sherbet, softened
1 pt. lime sherbet, softened
12-oz. container frozen whipped topping, thawed
Garnish: gumdrops

Slice angel food cake crosswise to make 4 equal layers; place bottom layer on a serving plate. Spread orange sherbet evenly over the top; repeat with next 2 cake layers, using raspberry and lime sherbet. Top with final cake layer; frost with whipped topping. Freeze until firm, about one hour. Garnish with gumdrops before serving. Serves 12 to 15.

Margie Williams
Gooseberry Patch

Ice Cream Roll

Made like a traditional pumpkin roll, but it's a chocolatey ice cream-filled cake.

tasty twist

Double up on the chocolate flavor and use chocolate ice cream.

4 eggs, separated
¾ c. sugar
1 t. vanilla extract
¾ c. cake flour
¼ c. baking cocoa
¾ t. baking powder
¼ t. salt
powdered sugar
3 c. ice cream, softened
Garnish: chocolate syrup

Beat egg yolks in a large bowl until light and fluffy, about 3 minutes; gradually add sugar and vanilla. Blend well; set aside. Mix flour, cocoa, baking powder and salt in a separate bowl; slowly add to egg mixture. Add egg whites; spread batter evenly in a greased and floured wax paper-lined 15"x10" jelly-roll pan. Bake at 350 degrees for 15 minutes; turn out onto a tea towel dusted with powdered sugar. Peel off wax paper; roll up cake and towel. Let cool 30 minutes; unroll cake. Spread with ice cream; roll up again, without the towel. Cover with plastic wrap; freeze until firm. Slice and drizzle with chocolate syrup before serving. Serves 18.

Jeanne Heykoop
Fostoria, OH

Coconut Freezer Cake

18¼-oz. pkg. white cake mix

14-oz. pkg. sweetened flaked coconut

16-oz. container sour cream

2 c. sugar

8-oz. container frozen whipped topping, thawed

Prepare cake mix according to package directions, dividing batter evenly among 3 greased 9" round cake pans. Bake according to package directions. Let cool. Combine coconut, sour cream and sugar in a large bowl; set aside one cup of mixture. Place one cake layer on a cake stand and spread half the remaining coconut mixture on top. Repeat with second cake layer and coconut mixture. Top with third cake layer; set aside. Combine reserved coconut mixture with whipped topping in a bowl; frost top and sides of cake. Place in freezer. Let stand 15 minutes before serving. Serves 12 to 18.

Lemonade-Ice Cream Pie

tasty twist

Try substituting limeade or pink lemonade for a fresh new taste.

½ gal. vanilla ice cream or frozen yogurt, softened
12-oz. can frozen lemonade concentrate, thawed
16-oz. container frozen whipped topping, thawed and divided
2 9-inch graham cracker crusts, frozen
Garnish: lemon slices and mint sprigs

Mix ice cream or yogurt, lemonade and half of the whipped topping in a large bowl; divide and spread equally into pie crusts. Spread with remaining whipped topping; freeze, uncovered, until firm. Cover with plastic wrap and freeze an additional 4 hours. Garnish with lemon slices and mint sprigs before serving. Serves 16.

Cheryl Laufer
Chesterland, OH

Orange-Filled Napoleons

Easy to make and elegant to serve!

8-oz. pkg. frozen puff pastry sheets, thawed
2 c. vanilla ice cream, softened
1 navel orange, peeled and thinly sliced
powdered sugar

Unfold pastry and cut into 8 rectangles. Place on an ungreased baking sheet and bake at 375 degrees for 20 minutes, or until pastries are puffed and golden. Cool on a wire rack. To serve, split pastries lengthwise. Spoon ice cream on one half; top with orange slices and replace pastry top. Dust with powdered sugar and serve immediately. Serves 8.

Orange-Filled
Napoleons

Brownie-Ice Cream Pie

Whole strawberries dipped into melted chocolate make a beautiful garnish served alongside this tasty pie.

20-oz. pkg. double chocolate
    fudge brownie mix
2 eggs
½ c. oil
¼ c. water
⅔ c. semi-sweet chocolate
    chips

9-inch pie crust
Garnish: vanilla ice cream
    and strawberry ice cream
    topping

Combine brownie mix, eggs, oil and water in a large mixing bowl; stir until blended. Mix in chocolate chips; spoon into crust. Bake at 350 degrees for 40 to 45 minutes; cool completely. Serve pie wedges topped with a scoop of ice cream and strawberry ice cream topping. Serves 8.

Vickie
Gooseberry Patch

Frozen Mocha Dessert

This makes enough to serve a crowd!

2 t. instant coffee granules
1 T. hot water
1 c. crushed chocolate
   sandwich cookie crumbs
¾ c. chopped pecans, divided
¼ c. butter, melted
2 8-oz. pkgs. cream cheese,
   softened
14-oz. can sweetened
   condensed milk
½ c. chocolate syrup
8-oz. container frozen whipped
   topping, thawed

Dissolve coffee in hot water in a small bowl; set aside. Combine cookie crumbs, ½ cup pecans and butter in a mixing bowl; press into an ungreased 13"x9" baking pan. Beat cream cheese in a bowl until light and fluffy; add coffee mixture, milk and chocolate syrup. Fold in whipped topping; spread over crust. Sprinkle with remaining pecans; freeze. Serves 24.

Janet Miller
Lakewood, CA

make-ahead magic

Make this crowd-pleaser up to 2 days ahead.

fun for the kids

A simple treat…dip banana slices in melted chocolate and roll in mini chocolate chips. Place on a baking sheet and freeze to make a frosty snack.

Crunchy Dessert

Crunchy Dessert

With its butter-pecan flavor and crisp cereal crunch, this dish will have everyone asking for seconds.

½ c. margarine
1 c. brown sugar, packed
2½ c. bite-size crispy rice cereal squares, crushed
3½ c. flaked coconut
½ c. chopped pecans
½ gal. vanilla ice cream

Melt margarine and brown sugar together in a 10" skillet over medium heat; add cereal, coconut and pecans. Toast until lightly brown and crisp, stirring constantly. Spread half the mixture in a greased 11"x9" baking pan; set aside. Remove ice cream from carton; cut into ½-inch slices. Arrange slices over toasted cereal mixture; seal edges of ice cream together with a spatula. Sprinkle with remaining toasted cereal mixture; cover and freeze until ready to serve. Cut into squares with a knife warmed by running hot water over it. Serves 20.

Lucinda Lewis
Brownstown, IN

Ice Cream Bar Dessert

12 ice cream sandwiches
11-oz. jar hot fudge sauce
12-oz. pkg. salted peanuts
12-oz. jar caramel topping
8-oz. container frozen whipped topping, thawed

Arrange ice cream sandwiches to cover the bottom of a 13"x9" freezer-safe pan; spread with a layer of hot fudge sauce. Sprinkle peanuts over the top; spread with caramel topping. Cover caramel with a layer of whipped topping; freeze. Slice into squares to serve. Serves 24.

Karen Cary
Marshalltown, IA

"My sister-in-law Kim shared this with me... great for a crowd!"
—Karen

Orange Sherbet Dessert

Crunchy walnuts and macaroons between two creamy layers of sherbet...yum!

½ gal. orange sherbet,
    softened and divided
1½ c. macaroon cookies,
    crushed
1 pt. whipping cream,
    whipped

1 c. chopped walnuts
1 t. vanilla extract
½ c. sugar

Spread half the orange sherbet in an ungreased 13"x9" glass baking pan; freeze until firm. Combine cookie crumbs, whipped cream, nuts, vanilla and sugar in a bowl; spread over frozen sherbet. Freeze again, until firm. Spread remaining orange sherbet over the top; freeze until firm. Cut into squares to serve. Serves 24 to 30.

Jennifer Brown
Hillsboro, OR

Velvety Lime Squares

A variety of ingredients come together to make this spectacular dessert. You'll agree…it's a hit!

3-oz. can flaked coconut, divided
2 c. vanilla wafer crumbs
2 T. butter, melted
2 T. sugar
2 3-oz. pkgs. lime gelatin mix
2 c. boiling water
6-oz. can frozen limeade concentrate
3 pts. vanilla ice cream, softened
⅛ t. salt
3 drops green food coloring
Optional: slivered almonds

kitchen tip

Allow the frozen limeade concentrate to thaw before stirring.

Spread ½ cup coconut on a baking sheet; toast at 375 degrees until lightly golden, about 5 minutes. Set aside. Combine remaining coconut, vanilla wafer crumbs, butter and sugar in a bowl; press into an ungreased 11"x7" baking pan. Bake at 375 degrees for 6 to 7 minutes; cool. Dissolve gelatin in boiling water; add limeade, ice cream, salt and food coloring, stirring until smooth. Pour into crust; sprinkle with toasted coconut and almonds, if desired. Cover tightly; freeze until firm. Let stand at room temperature 20 minutes; cut into squares to serve. Serves 15.

Kathy Unruh
Fresno, CA

Frozen Fruitcake Dessert

Spoon into individual serving cups if you'd like.

1 c. sour cream
½ c. sugar
2 T. lemon juice
1 t. vanilla extract
4½-oz. container frozen whipped topping, divided
13-oz. can crushed pineapple, drained
½ c. candied red cherries, chopped
½ c. candied green cherries, chopped
½ c. chopped walnuts

Blend sour cream, sugar, lemon juice, vanilla and half the whipped topping in a large mixing bowl; refrigerate remaining whipped topping for use in another recipe. Fold in remaining ingredients; spread into a 13"x9" freezer-safe pan; freeze. Cut into squares to serve. Serves 8 to 10.

Faye Davis
Owingsville, KY

tasty twist

Serve this at Christmas for a fun take on traditional fruitcake.

Coffee Cream Parfaits

Sprinkle chocolate curls on top for an extra treat!

1 qt. vanilla ice cream, slightly thawed
1 c. coffee liqueur
½ c. whipping cream
1½ t. sugar
1½ t. instant espresso granules

In tall ice cream or parfait glasses, layer the ice cream and liqueur. Chill in freezer for half an hour or more. When ready to serve, whip together cream, sugar and espresso until soft peaks form; top parfaits. Serves 4.

Easy Ice Cream Treats

Barbara Spilsbury (Hacienda Heights, CA)

Even the kids can make this!

18½-oz. pkg. chocolate cake mix   4 c. vanilla ice cream, softened

Prepare cake mix according to package directions, omitting eggs. Drop by heaping tablespoonfuls onto greased baking sheets; bake at 350 degrees for 15 minutes. Cool completely. Spread ice cream on the flat bottom side of half the cookies; top with remaining cookies, bottom-side down. Gently press to form a sandwich; wrap individually and freeze. Serves 6.

Snowballs
Tina Stidam (Ashley, OH)

With this recipe, it's easy to enjoy a snowball on a hot summer day!

1 qt. vanilla ice cream
2½ c. flaked coconut

Optional: chocolate syrup

Scoop large rounded scoops of ice cream; roll in coconut. Lightly pat coconut into ice cream; place on a wax paper-lined baking sheet. Cover with plastic wrap; freeze at least 2 hours. Drizzle with chocolate syrup before serving, if desired. Serves 4 to 6.

Chocolatey Ice Cream Cookies

Round, chocolatey, ice cream-filled treats!

1 c. butter, softened
1¼ c. powdered sugar
4 egg yolks
2 t. vanilla extract
2 1-oz. sqs. unsweetened
   baking chocolate, melted

3 c. all-purpose flour
1 qt. ice cream, softened
Optional: powdered sugar

Blend butter and powdered sugar in a large bowl; add egg yolks, vanilla and chocolate. Blend well; mix in flour. Divide dough into quarters; shape each quarter into a log, 1½ inches in diameter. Wrap in plastic wrap; refrigerate until firm, about 30 minutes. Slice rolls into ⅛-inch thick slices; place 2 inches apart on parchment paper-lined baking sheets. Bake at 350 degrees for 8 to 10 minutes; remove to wire racks. Cool completely; dust with powdered sugar, if desired. Spread several tablespoons ice cream on flat bottom side of half the cookies; top with remaining cookies, bottom-side down, to form sandwiches. Serve immediately. Makes about 4 dozen.

Rita Morgan
Pueblo, CO

quick fix idea

Cake doughnuts make a yummy ice cream sandwich. Cut the doughnut in half and add a scoop of softened ice cream between the two halves. Place on a baking sheet and freeze one hour...tasty!

Coconut-Almond Dream

Ice cream tucked between crispy, sweet layers of coconut, almonds and brown sugar...decadent!

tasty twist

Lightly toast the flaked coconut for a nutty flavor.

2½ c. puffed rice cereal
1 c. brown sugar, packed
1 c. flaked coconut
1½ c. sliced almonds

½ c. butter, melted
½ gal. vanilla ice cream, softened

Combine cereal, brown sugar, coconut, almonds and butter in a bowl; press half of mixture into a 13"x9" baking pan. Spread with ice cream; layer remaining cereal mixture over ice cream. Freeze until set. Cut into squares to serve. Serves 15.

Donna Kidd
Bradley, IL

Ice Cream Thumbprints

A delicious twist on a childhood favorite.

2 c. butter, softened
3½ to 4 c. all-purpose flour
1 pt. vanilla ice cream, softened

Garnish: favorite fruit or nut filling, powdered sugar

Work butter into flour with your hands in a large bowl; gradually mix in ice cream. Combine thoroughly; shape dough into one-inch balls. Place on ungreased baking sheets; flatten slightly. Lightly press thumb in center of each cookie, forming a depression; spoon desired filling into depression. Bake at 350 degrees for 20 to 25 minutes, until golden. Cool; sprinkle with powdered sugar. Makes 3 to 4 dozen.

Kris Erdman
Chicago, IL

Double Chocolate Ice Cream

Try using white or dark chocolate-covered sandwich cookies for even more chocolatey goodness.

2 6-oz. pkgs. chocolate
    pudding mix
3 qts. half-and-half, divided

2 c. crushed chocolate
    sandwich cookie crumbs
12-oz. can evaporated milk

Heat pudding mix and 2 quarts half-and-half in a saucepan over medium heat until thickened; chill overnight. Pour into a 3-quart ice cream maker; add remaining half-and-half, crushed cookies and enough evaporated milk to reach the fill line. Freeze according to directions on ice cream maker. Makes 3 quarts.

Carrie Padgett
Madera, CA

tasty twist

For a ghoulish treat, mix gummy worms into the ice cream before freezing.

dig in the dirt

Dirt for dessert? Here's a fun serving idea! Line the inside of a new clay pot with wax paper and then fill with softened ice cream. Cover the ice cream with crushed chocolate cookies and slip a pinwheel in the center. Everyone will love eating their "dirt"!

Orange Sherbet Ice Cream

Only 2 ingredients...wow!

14-oz. can sweetened
condensed milk

2 ltr. orange soda

Combine milk and soda in an ice cream maker; freeze according to ice cream maker's instructions. Makes about 2 quarts.

Debbie Crawford
Strafford, MO

tasty twist

Add your favorite stir-ins such as chocolate chips, nuts and chopped candies.

Classic Vanilla Ice Cream

A basic, old-fashioned recipe that never fails.

1½ c. whipping cream
1½ c. milk
6 egg yolks

2 T. vanilla extract
½ c. sugar
¼ t. salt

Combine whipping cream and milk in a heavy saucepan over medium heat until steam rises; remove from heat and set aside. Blend egg yolks, vanilla, sugar and salt in a bowl until smooth; gradually pour into warm cream mixture. Cook over medium-low heat; stir constantly until thick, about 6 minutes. Do not boil. Pour through a sieve into a bowl; refrigerate one hour. Freeze according to ice cream maker's instructions. Serves 4 to 6.

Teresa Beal
Gooseberry Patch

Creamsicles

1 pt. vanilla ice cream or ice
   milk, softened
6-oz. can frozen orange juice
   concentrate, thawed

¼ c. honey
1½ c. fat-free milk

Mix together ice cream, orange juice concentrate and honey in a large
bowl. Gradually beat in milk. Freeze in small wax paper cups or in an ice
cube tray. Insert sticks in paper cup molds when partially frozen. Makes
one dozen.

Banana Split Ice Cream

Try this…you'll love it!

tasty twist

Don't forget the whipped cream when ready to serve.

5 c. milk, divided
4 egg yolks
2 14-oz. cans sweetened
   condensed milk
2 c. bananas, mashed
2 T. lime juice

2½ T. vanilla extract
¾ c. chocolate syrup
½ c. chopped pecans, toasted
⅓ c. maraschino cherries,
   halved

Combine 2½ cups milk and egg yolks in a heavy saucepan; stir well with a whisk. Cook over medium heat 10 minutes, or until mixture thickens and coats a spoon; stir constantly. Do not let boil; remove from heat. Pour egg yolk mixture, remaining milk and condensed milk into a large mixing bowl; stir well. Cover; chill completely. Add bananas, lime juice and vanilla; blend well. Pour into an ice cream maker; freeze according to manufacturer's directions. Spoon ice cream into a 13"x9" freezer-safe pan; allow to soften. Gently fold in syrup, pecans and cherries; cover and freeze 2 hours, or until firm. Serves 24.

Janet Pastrick
Gooseberry Patch

kid-friendly treat

Make banana splits easier for little fingers to pick up. Instead of slicing the bananas lengthwise, slice them into circles and then top with ice cream, hot fudge and whipped cream.

Butter-Pecan Ice Cream

What is it about this classic that makes it so popular? It seems no one can resist the combination of brown sugar and pecans.

1 c. chopped pecans
½ c. sugar
2 T. butter
4 c. half-and-half

2 c. brown sugar, packed
4 t. vanilla extract
4 c. whipping cream

Combine pecans, sugar and butter in a heavy 8" skillet; stir constantly over medium heat until sugar dissolves and caramelizes, about 6 to 8 minutes. Remove from heat; spread nuts on a buttered baking sheet and separate into clusters. Set aside; cool completely. Combine half-and-half, brown sugar and vanilla in a large mixing bowl; stir until sugar dissolves. Fold in pecan mixture and whipping cream; freeze in a 4- or 5-quart ice cream maker according to manufacturer's directions. Once ice cream has formed, freeze another 4 hours before serving. Makes about 3½ quarts.

Marla Caldwell
Forest, IN

Best-Ever Vanilla Ice Cream

There's nothing like homemade ice cream. This is just a basic vanilla recipe, great by itself or with some fresh fruit added.

2 qts. half-and-half
½ pt. whipping cream
1½ c. sugar

5 t. vanilla extract
2 t. salt

Mix all ingredients in a large bowl; freeze in an ice cream maker according to manufacturer's directions. Makes one gallon.

Wendy Jacobs
Idaho Falls, ID

Pumpkin Ice Cream

Just for fun, serve this in hollowed-out mini pumpkins!

1 c. canned pumpkin
¼ t. pumpkin pie spice

1 qt. vanilla ice cream, softened
Garnish: gingersnaps

Combine pumpkin and pumpkin pie spice in a large freezer-safe container; stir in ice cream until well blended. Freeze until hardened; serve with gingersnaps. Serves 4 to 6.

Sandi Grock
Huntsville, TX

Fresh Peach Ice Cream

This low-fat, creamy recipe tastes very rich…it brings back memories of summer on the farm. Garnish with fresh mint.

5 c. low-fat milk, divided
4 egg yolks
8 ripe peaches, peeled and mashed
2 T. freshly squeezed lemon juice

2½ T. vanilla extract
½ t. ground ginger
½ t. almond extract
2 14-oz. cans fat-free sweetened condensed milk

Combine 2½ cups of the milk and the egg yolks in a heavy saucepan and whisk well. Cook and stir over medium heat about 10 minutes, or until mixture coats a spoon. (Do not overcook, or it will turn into scrambled eggs!) Combine egg mixture with remaining milk, peaches and all remaining ingredients in a large bowl and stir well. Cover and chill. Pour mixture into an ice cream maker. Freeze according to manufacturer's directions. Spoon into a container with a tight-fitting lid and freeze one hour, or until completely firm. Serves 12 to 24.

Apricot Sundaes

Your favorite vanilla ice cream serves as a base for this delicious fruity sundae.

12-oz. jar apricot preserves
1½ t. lemon zest
⅓ c. unsweetened pineapple juice
⅓ c. brown sugar, firmly packed
vanilla ice cream

Combine all ingredients except ice cream in a microwave-safe bowl and microwave on high 2 minutes. Stir until sugar is dissolved. Serve warm over vanilla ice cream. Serves 6.

Country-Style Vanilla Ice Cream

Bring the country fair to your kids any time of year...set up an ice cream stand right in the kitchen. Get out the sprinkles, jimmies, hot fudge and caramel sauces, maraschino cherries and nuts. Yum!

4 eggs
2½ c. sugar
2 T. vanilla extract
¼ t. salt
4 c. whipping cream
5 c. milk

Beat eggs in a mixing bowl until foamy; gradually blend in sugar, vanilla and salt. Mix until thickened; set aside. Combine whipping cream and milk in a saucepan over medium heat; cook until steam rises from the pan. Blend in egg mixture; cook 5 more minutes. Bring to room temperature; refrigerate at least one hour. Pour into an ice cream maker; freeze according to manufacturer's directions. Makes 4 quarts.

Kristina Wyatt
Madera, CA

Easy Strawberry Ice Cream

Serve with a ripe red strawberry and a wafer cookie. Vary the recipe with different fruits throughout the summer.

⅔ c. very cold buttermilk
1 t. orange extract

2 10-oz. pkgs. frozen
  strawberries, slightly thawed

Place buttermilk and orange extract in a blender or food processor. Cut slightly thawed fruit into chunks and add to blender. Blend until mixture is smooth and the consistency of ice cream. Serve immediately. Serves 6.

Frozen Cherry Yogurt

Frozen yogurt's a snap to make…give it a try!

4 c. fresh or frozen dark,
  sweet cherries, pitted,
  thawed and divided
8 c. plain yogurt

2 c. whipping cream
1¼ c. sugar
2 T. vanilla extract

Purée half of the cherries in a blender; set aside remaining whole cherries. Combine puréed cherries with yogurt, whipping cream, sugar and vanilla in a large bowl; cover and refrigerate 30 minutes. Freeze in an ice cream maker according to manufacturer's directions; transfer to a freezer-safe bowl. Let stand to soften. Stir in remaining cherries; refreeze until hardened. Makes 4 quarts.

Megan Brooks
Antioch, TN

Frozen Peach Yogurt

1 env. unflavored gelatin
1 c. milk
½ c. sugar
1 t. salt
2½ c. vanilla yogurt
2 t. vanilla extract
3 c. peaches, pitted, peeled
and puréed

Sprinkle gelatin over milk in a saucepan; let stand one minute. Heat over low heat until gelatin is dissolved, stirring constantly; remove from heat. Add sugar and salt; stir to dissolve. Mix in yogurt, vanilla and peaches; cover and chill. Pour into an ice cream maker; freeze according to manufacturer's directions. Serves 4 to 6.

Gretchen Miller
Kearney, MO

Apricot Sherbet

2 qts. apricots, peeled and
pitted
1½ c. sugar
1 t. lemon juice

Place apricots, a few at a time, in a blender; blend until smooth and creamy. Repeat until blended mixture equals one quart; add sugar and lemon juice. Blend well; freeze. Serves 4.

LaVerne Fang
Joliet, IL

kitchen tip

Substitute nectarines or peaches for a refreshing treat.

Coffee Sherbet

⅔ c. sugar
4 c. strong coffee, hot and
freshly brewed
½ c. milk

Combine sugar and hot coffee in a bowl until sugar dissolves. Add milk and chill thoroughly. Freeze in an ice cream maker according to manufacturer's directions. Serve immediately. Serves 8.

Pineapple Sherbet

Make your own sherbet…oh-so simple!

1 qt. milk
1½ c. sugar

½ c. lemon juice
1 c. crushed pineapple

Scald milk in a saucepan over medium heat; cool. Add sugar, lemon juice and pineapple; blend well. Freeze in an ice cream maker according to manufacturer's instructions. Makes 2 quarts.

Classic Chocolate Shakes

Classic Chocolate Shakes

Brings back the days of ice cream parlors and dime-store counters. Garnish with whipped topping and a cherry.

1½ c. sugar
1 c. water
½ c. baking cocoa

1 t. vanilla extract
¼ c. whole milk
6 c. natural vanilla ice cream

Combine sugar and water in a heavy saucepan and stir over medium-low heat until sugar is completely dissolved. Increase heat and bring to a boil. Place cocoa in a bowl and gradually whisk in sugar syrup. Return mixture to saucepan and boil one minute, continuing to whisk. Whisk in vanilla, pour into bowl immediately and allow to cool completely. Chill, covered, at least one hour. For each milkshake, pour 3 tablespoons syrup and one tablespoon milk into a blender. Add 1½ cups ice cream and blend until smooth. Pour into a tall glass and serve with a big paper straw. Serves 4.

kitchen tip

Look for old-fashioned milkshake glasses to serve this parlor treat.

Deluxe Ice Cream Sandwiches

We like these chewy, thin oatmeal cookies.

1½ c. butter
3 c. uncooked rolled oats (not instant)
1½ T. all-purpose flour
1 t. salt
1¾ c. sugar

2 t. vanilla extract
2 eggs, lightly beaten
½ gal. natural vanilla ice cream
candy sprinkles

Melt butter in a large saucepan over low heat. Let cool and add oats, flour, salt, sugar and vanilla. Stir well to combine, then add eggs and mix thoroughly. Spoon batter by 1½ tablespoons about 3 inches apart onto a buttered parchment paper-lined baking sheet. Flatten cookies into circles. Bake at 350 degrees for about 15 minutes, or until golden. Let cool. Unwrap a square block of vanilla ice cream and slice into one-inch thick slices, cutting into squares big enough to slightly overlap edges of cookies. Sandwich ice cream between cookies. Dip edges of sandwiches into sprinkles. Wrap individually and freeze until ready to serve. Makes one dozen.

Chocolatey Popsicles

Kids will love these frozen treats!

3½-oz. pkg. instant chocolate pudding mix

½ c. sugar
3 c. milk

Prepare chocolate pudding according to package directions; set aside. Combine sugar and milk in a medium mixing bowl; stir in pudding and blend until smooth. Pour mixture into small plastic cups or popsicle molds and freeze. When partially set, insert a popsicle stick; refreeze. Makes 8.

Beth Kramer
Port Saint Lucie, FL

Homemade Ice Cream in a Bag

Need a classroom treat? This works. Remember the spoons so that the ice cream can be eaten right out of the bag.

1 c. milk
1 T. sugar
1 t. vanilla extract
1-pt. plastic zipping bag
½-gal. plastic zipping bag

ice
½ c. rock salt
Garnish: flavored syrup or candy sprinkles

Pour milk, sugar and vanilla into a pint-size bag; seal. Fill larger bag halfway full with ice; pour rock salt on top. Place small bag inside large bag; seal large bag. Shake bag 10 to 15 minutes, until ice cream forms; remove small bag and rinse under cold water. Garnish with flavored syrup or sprinkles. Serves one.

Stefanie Schroeder
Bay City, TX

Raspberry Pops

Try making these pops with blackberries or strawberries for a nice variety!

¼ c. honey
8-oz. pkg. cream cheese,
  softened
1 c. bananas, sliced
10-oz. pkg. frozen raspberries,
  slightly thawed

1 c. whipping cream, whipped
2 c. mini marshmallows
10 5-oz. paper drinking cups
10 wooden treat sticks

Gradually add honey to cream cheese in a bowl, mixing until well blended. Stir in fruit; fold in whipped cream and marshmallows. Pour into paper cups; insert a wooden stick in the center of each and freeze until firm. Peel away cups and enjoy. Makes 10.

Wild Blueberry Ice

Wild Blueberry Ice

¼ c. sugar
½ c. water

15-oz. pkg. frozen blueberries in heavy syrup, thawed and syrup drained (reserve syrup)

Cook sugar and water in a small saucepan over low heat until sugar dissolves. Remove from heat; add syrup from blueberries and half of the berries. Chill thoroughly. Freeze mixture in an ice cream maker according to manufacturer's directions. Serve immediately, topped with remaining blueberries. Serves 6.

kitchen tip

Frozen blueberries make for easy preparation…but you can also use fresh blueberries that you have simmered and stirred in a small amount of water and allowed to cool.

Honeydew Sorbet

You can also make this recipe with cantaloupe. Delicious!

2 lbs. honeydew melon, peeled and seeded
½ c. sweet dessert wine

½ c. sugar
¼ t. cinnamon

Cut melon into large pieces and purée in a blender. Add wine, sugar and cinnamon and blend until sugar dissolves. Pour mixture into an ice cream maker and freeze according to manufacturer's directions. Freeze in a tightly covered container. Serves 6.

METRIC EQUIVALENTS

The recipes that appear in this cookbook use the standard U.S. method for measuring liquid and dry or solid ingredients (teaspoons, tablespoons and cups). The information in the following charts is provided to help cooks outside the United States successfully use these recipes. All equivalents are approximate.

METRIC EQUIVALENTS FOR DIFFERENT TYPES OF INGREDIENTS

A standard cup measure of a dry or solid ingredient will vary in weight depending on the type of ingredient.
A standard cup of liquid is the same volume for any type of liquid. Use the following chart when converting standard cup measures to grams (weight) or milliliters (volume).

Standard Cup	Fine Powder (ex. flour)	Grain (ex. rice)	Granular (ex. sugar)	Liquid Solids (ex. butter)	Liquid (ex. milk)
1	140 g	150 g	190 g	200 g	240 ml
¾	105 g	113 g	143 g	150 g	180 ml
⅔	93 g	100 g	125 g	133 g	160 ml
½	70 g	75 g	95 g	100 g	120 ml
⅓	47 g	50 g	63 g	67 g	80 ml
¼	35 g	38 g	48 g	50 g	60 ml
⅛	18 g	19 g	24 g	25 g	30 ml

USEFUL EQUIVALENTS FOR LIQUID INGREDIENTS BY VOLUME

¼ tsp	=						1 ml
½ tsp	=						2 ml
1 tsp	=						5 ml
3 tsp	=	1 Tbsp		= ½ fl oz	=	15 ml	
		2 Tbsp	= ⅛ c	= 1 fl oz	=	30 ml	
		4 Tbsp	= ¼ c	= 2 fl oz	=	60 ml	
		5⅓ Tbsp	= ⅓ c	= 3 fl oz	=	80 ml	
		8 Tbsp	= ½ c	= 4 fl oz	=	120 ml	
		10⅔ Tbsp	= ⅔ c	= 5 fl oz	=	160 ml	
		12 Tbsp	= ¾ c	= 6 fl oz	=	180 ml	
		16 Tbsp	= 1 c	= 8 fl oz	=	240 ml	
		1 pt	= 2 c	= 16 fl oz	=	480 ml	
		1 qt	= 4 c	= 32 fl oz	=	960 ml	
				33 fl oz	=	1000 ml	= 1 liter

USEFUL EQUIVALENTS FOR DRY INGREDIENTS BY WEIGHT

(To convert ounces to grams, multiply the number of ounces by 30.)

1 oz	=	¹⁄₁₆ lb	=	30 g
4 oz	=	¼ lb	=	120 g
8 oz	=	½ lb	=	240 g
12 oz	=	¾ lb	=	360 g
16 oz	=	1 lb	=	480 g

USEFUL EQUIVALENTS FOR LENGTH

(To convert inches to centimeters, multiply the number of inches by 2.5.)

1 in			=	2.5 cm	
6 in	= ½ ft		=	15 cm	
12 in	= 1 ft		=	30 cm	
36 in	= 3 ft	= 1 yd	=	90 cm	
40 in			=	100 cm	= 1 meter

USEFUL EQUIVALENTS FOR COOKING/OVEN TEMPERATURES

	Fahrenheit	Celsius	Gas Mark
Freeze Water	32° F	0° C	
Room Temperature	68° F	20° C	
Boil Water	212° F	100° C	
Bake	325° F	160° C	3
	350° F	180° C	4
	375° F	190° C	5
	400° F	200° C	6
	425° F	220° C	7
	450° F	230° C	8
Broil			Grill

index

bread puddings & custards

Baked Custard, 211
Black Bottom Pudding, 204
Bragging-Rights Banana
    Pudding, 203
Brownie Pudding Trifle, 211
Chocolate Lover's Bread
    Pudding, 188
Christmas Date Pudding, 206
Christmas Plum Pudding, 207
Cinnamon Bread Pudding, 188
Creamy Pear Bread Pudding, 187
Delicious Custard Cake
    Pudding, 209
English Bread Pudding, 195
Family-Style Chocolate Pudding
    Mix, 198
Favorite Vanilla Pudding Mix, 198
French Apple Bread Pudding, 192
Grandpa's Bread Pudding, 197
Granny Christian's Biscuit
    Pudding, 194
Hot Cinnamon Pudding, 201
Just Peachy Bread Pudding, 190
Lemon Pudding, 208
Lemony Bread Pudding, 186
Maple Bread Pudding, 194
Miss Piggy Pudding, 212
Mocha-Chocolate Steamed
    Pudding, 193
Old-Fashioned Bread
    Pudding, 196

Old-Fashioned Chocolate
    Pudding, 192
Raisin Bread Pudding, 197
Raisin Bread Pudding & Vanilla
    Sauce, 205
Rose's Baked Custard, 212
Slow-Cooker Tapioca
    Pudding, 201
Texas-Style Bread Pudding, 190
Tropical Pineapple Pudding, 191
Upside-Down Date Pudding, 202

breads & coffee cakes

Anadama Bread, 171
Applechip Coffee Cake, 158
Apple-Oatmeal Coffee Cake, 152
Banana & Walnut Bread, 162
Blueberry Cream Coffee
    Cake, 157
Cheddar Quick Bread, 180
Cherry-Chip Bread, 158
Cherry Coffee Cake, 153
Chocolate-Zucchini Bread, 164
Cinnamon Twist Bread, 161
Coffee Cake Crescents, 151
Coffee-Can Molasses Bread, 166
Country Cheddar Loaf, 175
Dilly Bread, 180
English Muffin Loaf, 170
Farmhouse Buttermilk Bread, 172
Focaccia, 178
Fruit Coffee Cake, 156
Glazed Lemon Bread, 165

Granny's Country Cornbread, 182
Irish Soda Bread, 173
Mediterranean Loaf, 179
Old-Fashioned Honey Bread, 168
Old-World Black Bread, 177
Onion & Sour Cream Bread, 175
Orange-Nut Bread, 160
Peanut Butter Bread, 163
Pennsylvania Dutch Loaves, 167
Pesto Marbled Bread, 179
Quick Sourdough Bread, 182
Raspberry Coffee Cake, 155
Sour Cream-Cinnamon Coffee
   Cake, 148
Spicy Buttermilk Coffee Cake, 150
Spoonbread, 183
Strawberry Bread, 162
Sugar-Topped Coffee Cake, 149

Sweet Corn-Buttermilk
   Bread, 173
Vermont Graham Bread, 164
Walnut and Pumpkin Bread, 161
Whole-Wheat Bread, 176

cakes

Angel Food Cake, 31
Blue-Ribbon Chocolate Cake, 14
Boston Cream Cake, 10
Brown Sugar Pound Cake, 30
Caramel Cake, 13
Cherry-Chocolate Marble
   Cake, 30
Chocolate-Chip Cheesecake, 46
Chocolate-Pumpkin Pound
   Cake, 39

Classic Cheesecake, 53
Cookie Dough Cheesecake, 48
Creamy Amaretto Cheesecake, 46
Double-Chocolate Mousse
   Cake, 17
Éclair Cake, 15
Fudge Cake, 38
Harvest Apple Cheesecake, 51
Honey Bun Cake, 21
Italian Cream Cake, 27
Mandarin Orange Cake, 19
Nana's Famous Coconut-Pineapple
   Cake, 16
No-Bake Cheesecake, 54
No-Bake Strawberry
   Cheesecake, 54
Nobby Apple Cake, 36
Nutty Raisin Cake, 44
Oatmeal Cake, 20
Old-Fashioned Jam Cake, 18
Peanut Butter Sheet Cake, 45
Praline-Cream Cheese Pound
   Cake, 40
Praline Pound Cake, 29
Raspberry Crunch Cheesecake, 52
Raspberry Truffle Cheesecake, 57
Raspberry Upside-Down Cake, 35
Red Velvet Cake, 11
Rich Spice Cake, 32
Root Beer Cake, 37
Strawberry Layer Cake, 8
Strawberry Shortcake, 22
Summertime Strawberry
   Shortcake, 33
Texas Sheet Cake, 25
Three-Layer Chocolate Cake, 26
Toffee & Black Walnut Cake, 43
Tutti-Frutti Cake, 44
Vanilla Wafer Cake, 35
Warm Turtle Cake, 22

cookies & bars

Banana Bars, 90
Birthday Brownies, 99
Butterscotch Cookies, 65
Cappuccino Brownies, 101
Caramel Brownies, 99
Chewy Chocolate-Caramel
    Bars, 88
Chewy Chocolate Cookies, 70
Chocolate-Butter Cream
    Squares, 95
Chocolate Chip-Raisin
    Cookies, 73
Chocolate-Raspberry
    Brownies, 100
Chocolate Thumbprint
    Cookies, 71
Clothespin Cookies, 81
Coffee-Toffee Bars, 89
Crème de Menthe Cookies, 86
Frosted Orange Cookies, 75
Frosted Sugar Cookies, 77
Fudgy Oatmeal Bars, 93
Fudgy-Topped Brownies, 96
Grandmother's Oatmeal Bars, 91
Gumdrop Cookies, 78
Honey-Pecan Bars, 87
Honey & Spice Cookies, 66
Hucklebucks, 82
Maple Drop Cookies, 60
Melt-in-Your-Mouth Cookies, 80
Molasses Sugar Cookies, 63
No-Bake Cookies, 72
Oatmeal Crinkles, 70
Oatmeal-Raisin Spice Cookies, 60
Old-Fashioned Raspberry
    Cut-Outs, 75
Old-Time Icebox Cookies, 80
Peanut Butter Bars, 92

Peanut Butter Cookies, 65
Peanut Butter Jumbos, 74
Polka-Dot Cookies, 76
Raspberry-Coconut Bars, 90
Rocky Road Treats, 84
Snickerdoodles, 72
Soft Gingerbread Cookies, 69
Sour Cream-Apple Squares, 94
Spritz, 83
Thumbprint Cookies, 83
White Chocolate-Cranberry
    Cookies, 66
Whoopie Pies, 85

frozen treats

Apricot Sherbet, 242
Apricot Sundaes, 240
Banana Split Ice Cream, 236
Best-Ever Vanilla Ice Cream, 237
Brownie-Ice Cream Pie, 220

Butter-Pecan Ice Cream, 237
Chocolatey Ice Cream
    Cookies, 229
Chocolatey Popsicles, 246
Classic Chocolate Shakes, 245
Classic Vanilla Ice Cream, 234
Coconut-Almond Dream, 230
Coconut Freezer Cake, 217
Coffee Cream Parfaits, 226
Coffee Sherbet, 242
Country-Style Vanilla Ice
    Cream, 240
Creamsicles, 235
Crunchy Dessert, 223
Deluxe Ice Cream Sandwiches, 245
Double Chocolate Ice Cream, 233
Easy Ice Cream Treats, 227
Easy Strawberry Ice Cream, 241
Fresh Peach Ice Cream, 239
Frozen Cherry Yogurt, 241
Frozen Fruitcake Dessert, 226

Frozen Mocha Dessert, 221
Frozen Peach Yogurt, 242
Homemade Ice Cream in a
    Bag, 246
Honeydew Sorbet, 249
Ice Cream Bar Dessert, 223
Ice Cream Roll, 216
Ice Cream Thumbprints, 230
Lemonade-Ice Cream Pie, 218
Orange-Filled Napoleons, 218
Orange Sherbet Dessert, 224
Orange Sherbet Ice Cream, 234
Pineapple Sherbet, 243
Pumpkin Ice Cream, 238
Rainbow Sherbet Cake, 216
Raspberry Pops, 247
Snowballs, 228
Velvety Lime Squares, 225
Wild Blueberry Ice, 249

pies, cobblers & tarts

All-Star Cobbler, 126
Apple Brown Betty, 134
Apple-Cranberry Crisp, 135
Apple-Dapple Pie, 106
Autumn Apple Pie, 119
Blackberry Cobbler, 124
Brown Sugar Puddin' Pies, 113
Brown Sugar & Raisin Tarts, 137
Butterscotch Pie, 114
Buttery Blueberry Cobbler, 125
Caramel-Nut Tart, 138
Cherry Cobbler, 129
Chess Tarts, 136
Chestnut Farm Apple Crisp, 130
Chocolate-Butterscotch Pie, 105
Chocolate Tartlets, 136

Coconut-Caramel Crunch Pie,
    110
Coffee-Nut Torte, 141
Cookie Cobbler, 128
Crumbly Rhubarb Tart, 143
Crunchy Oat & Fruit Crisp, 132
Crunchy Peanut Butter Pie, 113
Crustless Pumpkin Pie, 114
Fresh Peach Pie, 122
Fudge Brownie Pie, 104
German Chocolate Pie, 105
Glazed Apple-Cream Pie, 115
Glazed Strawberry Tart, 144
Grandma Eddy's Apple
    Crumble, 132
Grandma's Easy Peach
    Cobbler, 129
Heartwarming Cherry Pie, 122
Luscious Blueberry Pie, 116
Mango Cobbler, 127
Maple-Pecan Pie, 107
Maple-Walnut Pie, 106
Mom's Rhubarb Pie, 123
Peanut Butter Strudel Pie, 109
Pear Pie, 120
Pecan Tarts, 134
Persimmon Crisp, 131
Pie Crust for Two-Crust Pie, 116
Raspberry Cobbler, 125
Raspberry-Cream Cheese Pie, 120
Rustic Peach Tart, 145
Rustic Pear Tart, 142
Sweet Potato Pie, 110
Triple-Berry Tart, 140